SHIPS IN FOCU
Decemb

C000286024

198279

CONTENTS

Ships in Focus Publications
Correspondence and editorial:
Roy Fenton
18 Durrington Avenue
London SW20 8NT
020 8879 3527
rfenton@rfenton.demon.co.uk

Orders and photographic:
John & Marion Clarkson
18 Franklands, Longton
Preston PR4 5PD
01772 612855
sales@shipsinfocus.co.uk
© 2002 Individual contributors, John Clarkson and Roy Fenton.

Printed by The Amadeus Press, Cleckheaton, Yorkshire.
Designed by Hugh Smallwood, John Clarkson and Roy Fenton.
SHIPS IN FOCUS RECORD
ISBN 1 901703 19 3

Thanks go to the readers who wr[c] *Record* 21 to assure us that the feature on Ellerman's *City of Oxford* class was about the right length. Indeed, response to this feature has been gratifying, and we will be having a full follow up in a forthcoming issue, when we will be tempted to extend coverage to the four ships of the closely-related *City of Birkenhead* class.

We are pleased to report that our request for further photographic features on ports has born fruit, and we have several lined up, which is not to say that more are unwelcome.

Continuing in the spirit of engaging in dialogue with our readers, we turn to one of those trivial-sounding issues that obsess editors, but are often barely remarked upon by the majority of readers. This issue is rotating pages, or perhaps we should say turning them sideways. It will not have escaped readers' notice that ships are long and thin, whilst the pages of *Record* are tall and narrow. On the numerous occasions when we have photographs whose quality and detail cries out for them to be displayed large, we have resorted to turning the page to achieve this. The alternative of running a photograph across two pages, and therefore over the gutter between the pages, is too awful to contemplate. We know that having to turn the whole journal through 90 degrees can be a bore (we have been told this twice by readers, or probably twice by one reader), so we aim to run such pages in sequence and when possible put them at the end of an issue. We also try to avoid having a caption on the opposite page which is at 90 degrees to the photograph. It is our editorial belief that having to rotate the page is a small price to pay for enjoying the added size of a full-page photograph, but if you disagree do let us know and we will review the issue.

John Clarkson   Roy Fenton

SUBSCRIPTION RATES FOR RECORD

Subscribers make a saving on postage, and receive each *Record* just as soon as it is published. They are also eligible for concessions on newly-published *Ships in Focus* titles. Readers can start their subscription with *any* issue, and are welcome to backdate it to receive previous issues.

	3 issues	6 issues	9 issues
UK	£23	£44	£63
Europe (airmail)	£25	£47	£68
Rest of world (surface mail)	£25	£47	£68
Rest of world (airmail)	£30	£56	£81

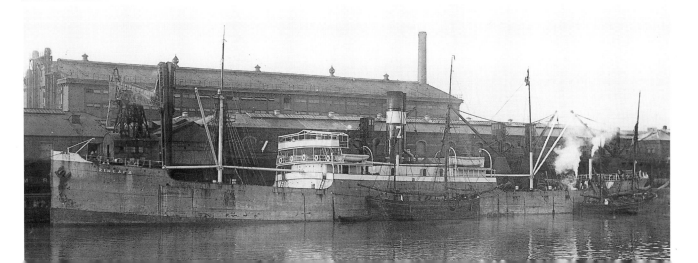

A view in later life of Turner, Brightman's *Zingara* which appears in a trials' shot on page 87. Comparison with this view shows the gaffs originally fitted have been removed, and she now has the more conventional Turner, Brightman tramp funnel, with the letter Z below the bands. *[J.& M. Clarkson]*

The Harland and Wolff motorship *Lochmonar* of 1923 at Vancouver. *[J. and M. Clarkson]*

Also built at Belfast was the *Drechtdijk,* one of the ships Holland America contributed to the North Pacific Coast Line. *[J. and M. Clarkson]*

Fleet in Focus
NORTH PACIFIC COAST LINE
David Burrell

The Panama Canal opened for traffic on 15th August 1914, with little fanfare in the shadow of war in Europe. But the potential was clear: North Pacific ports would be 5,500 miles closer to Europe than via Cape Horn. Outlets would open for North Pacific produce, timber, grain, fruit and minerals, which distance previously precluded. Ports like San Francisco, where the 1906 earthquake was still fresh in mind, would prosper. In Europe the first to take advantage of the new route in 1914 were the Harrison-Direct Line, East Asiatic Company and Johnston Line.

In London the Court of Directors of the Royal Mail Steam Packet Company, chaired by Sir Owen Philipps, later Lord Kylsant, with established West Indian and Central American interests, were keenly aware of the potential. The population of California, Oregon, Washington and British Columbia in 1900 was only 2.6 million. By 1990 it was over 40 million, an indication of the potential growth in trade.

Despite services to Cristobal and Colon from Southampton, New York and Caribbean ports, Royal Mail had no reason to immediately use the Canal. Only one of their ships transitted in 1914, on 5th November when *Jamaica* (1,138/1908) passed south to take up service on the West Coast. Previously employed in the Caribbean, she was being transferred to the affiliated Pacific Steam Navigation Company to replace their *Quito* (1,089/1888) which had had her passenger certificate withdrawn.

The Royal Mail connection to Vancouver was maintained by subsidiary Shire Line sailings through Suez to the Far East and across the Pacific. The attraction of Panama was clear and would have been adopted earlier but for the war. In 1920 agreement was reached with the Nederlandsch-Amerikaansche Stoomvaart Maatschappij (Holland America Line) to open a joint service. On 13 October the Court approved the following memorandum:

> "Arrangements have been made with Holland-America Line to run a joint freight Service between United Kingdom, Continent and North Pacific Ports via Panama Canal. The Dutch steamer *Moerdyk* inaugurates the Service and is scheduled to sail from London about 21st October. A three-weekly service will be established as soon as new tonnage is available.
> The RMSP steamers building for the Service are *Lochkatrine* and *Lochgoil*. The Holland-America Line are also building two steamers of a similar type. Until such time as these four Diesel steamers (sic) are ready, an intermittent Service will be run by other vessels of Holland-America Line.
> In connection with this development it will be necessary to open an Office of the Company in Seattle with a branch Office at Vancouver.
> 11th October, 1920"

First sailings

Royal Mail first advertised the service in November 1920, with *Eemdijk* (7,655/1914) to load mid-December. Holland America's first North Pacific sailing had been *Eemdijk,* sailing from Rotterdam on 7th July via New York and Philadelphia, followed by *Kinderdijk* (7,651/1914) direct from Rotterdam on 21st August 1920, and, under the agreement, *Moerdijk* (7,310/1914) on 13th

October and *Eemdijk* on 16th December. The first Royal Mail ship, *Lochkatrine,* sailed from Glasgow on 22nd January 1922.

The ships allocated to the service were augmented by others when needed, such as during the fruit season. They were part of large orders for motorships placed by Royal Mail during the war. A class of ten were delivered in 1920-24, five going to Glen Line (a Royal Mail subsidiary) as *Glenogle, Glengarry, Glenapp, Glenbeg* and *Glenshiel.* Royal Mail took three as *Lochkatrine, Lochgoil* and *Lochmonar,* Holland America named their pair *Dinteldijk* and *Drechtdijk. Lochkatrine* was the only one not built by Harland and Wolff, coming from the yard of John Brown and Co. Ltd. Six were built at Govan, birthplace of most early Harland and Wolff motorships. *Lochmonar* and *Glenshiel* were Belfast built, *Drechtdijk* Greenock.

They were amongst the largest motorships afloat. On an overall length of 502.0 feet, 62.3 feet beam and depths of 35.8 feet to awning and 29.6 feet to main decks, *Lochkatrine* was typical. Her tonnages were 9,419 gross, 5,812 nett and 11,580 deadweight. Two Harland and Wolff Burmeister & Wain-type diesels of 4,500 BHP gave a service speed of 12.5 knots. The bale capacity of 680,000 cubic feet included 144,000 cubic feet of refrigerated space (the Glen Line sisters' reefer capacity was only 40,000 cubic feet). Twelve passengers were catered for in the British ships, the Dutch pair carried 28. With a three island configuration and two decks below the awning deck, six holds and hatches were spread two forward, one in the split superstructure and three aft. The first launched, on 5th August 1921, was *Lochkatrine.* By June 1924 all five were in service.

The *Lochkatrine* in the Royal Albert Dock, London on 21st April 1935. *[National Maritime Museum P48441]*

Lochmonar was owned by subsidiary RMSP Meat Transports Ltd., formed in December 1914, rather than by the Royal Mail Steam Packet Company like her sisters. Along with *Asturias* (22,071/1925) and *Alcantara* (22,181/1926) she was built using borrowed funds guaranteed under the Trade Facilities Act and parallel Northern Ireland Loans Guarantee Act. Guarantees of £200,000 were given by the Treasury and £195,000 by the Ministry of Finance in Belfast. This borrowing required a mortgage be registered, but the Royal Mail charter did not permit giving a charge on assets, hence the setting up of a subsidiary company.

Loading ports in Europe were normally Rotterdam, Antwerp and London with alternate sailings by Royal Mail and Holland America taking different routes to Panama. Royal Mail ships called at Bermuda and Kingston, replacing a service dating from 1842, withdrawn in 1920. The Holland America ships sailed a more southerly route which replaced the old Spanish Main service. Cargo was transhipped to many Central American ports. On the North Pacific regular ports of call commenced with Los Angeles, San Francisco and up the coast to Portland, Vancouver and Victoria.

Casualty and collapse

The years until war again intervened saw the fleet working hard, with the normal operating problems. *Delftdijk* grounded homeward in the autumn of 1932, whilst *Lochgoil* grounded in 1923, had a cargo fire nearing Cristobal outward in May 1926 and a slight collision with the Swedish *Majfrid* (897/1922) on 12th July 1927 at Rotterdam. More serious, in January 1938 *Damsterdijk* ran down and sank the sailing barge *San Toy* in the Thames, with the loss of the barge crew. On 4th November 1924 *Cardiganshire* (9,426/1913), operating as an additional ship, sighted *Inspiration* (326/1917), dismasted on passage Pernambuco for St John's, Newfoundland, and took off the crew of the sinking schooner.

The major casualty was *Lochmonar*. Early on 30th November 1927 entering the Mersey by the Crosby Channel, from Vancouver, her steering gear failed. Before action could be taken she ran onto the revetment at Taylor's Bank and, the following day, broke her back. As she obstructed the fairway, the Mersey Dock and Harbour Board and the Liverpool and Glasgow Salvage Association discharged cargo and used explosives to sever the keel and release the aft section, still afloat in 80 feet of water. A week later the aft section was towed safely up river. In February 1928 this was towed to Belfast where a new 108 feet forward section was launched on 2nd August. Earlier, in December 1923, *Armagh* (12,269/1917) had been lost on Taylor's Bank revetment (see Ships in Focus *Record 3*, page 147), as was *Pegu* (8,183/1921) in November 1939 (*Record 4*, page 250).

September 1928 found eleven ships employed. Outward *Drechtdijk* had sailed from Rotterdam on the 11th and was reaching out into the Atlantic whilst *Eemdijk* was nearing the Canal. *Narenta* (8,236/1920) was sailing up the Pacific coast, following *Lochgoil* nearing her first discharge port. *Grootedijk* (8,365/1923) was discharging at Seattle. Homeward, *Lochmonar* was at Tacoma and *Noorderdijk* (8384/1913) at San Francisco. *Moerdijk* had sailed from Los Angeles for the Canal. *Dinteldijk* had left Cristobal for Europe, following *Kinderdijk* which was out in the Atlantic and *Lochkatrine* nearing Liverpool.

In 1930 Holland America added *Delftdijk* and *Damsterdijk* to the service, delivered by the Schiedam yard of Wilton-Fijenoord. Similar to the earlier ships, powered by Harland and Wolff diesels, they berthed 46 passengers. Royal Mail waited until 1937 to place an order with Harland and Wolff's Govan yard. Launched on 3rd March 1938 as *Lochavon*, she made her first sailing from Rotterdam on 6th August and brought the dedicated North Pacific Coast Line fleet to eight. They were to remain together for only a year before war dispersed them. Although not identified by nomenclature with the North Pacific, the refrigerated D-class built from 1942 to 1944 (*Deseado*, *Darro*, *Drina* and *Durango*) were designed for both the River Plate meat trade and the North Pacific run, providing ships to balance the Royal Mail contribution to the service with that of Holland America.

The major trauma of the Depression was the financial collapse of the Royal Mail Group, led by Lord Kylsant, one that led to the Companies Act, 1948. By this time in 1930 the loan raised to build *Lochmonar* had been repaid. Due to the size of the catastrophe and the financial repercusions, a salvage operation was undertaken by the Treasury, Bank of England and other creditors. Rather than a 'fire sale' of assets they were re-organised and floated as new companies. Hence in 1932 the North Pacific Coast Line passed to the newly formed Royal Mail Lines Ltd. In the meantime the service continued to operate.

The *Lochmonar* with her back broken on a training wall in the Mersey. The aft section, still in deep water, was salvaged.

[*J. and M. Clarkson*]

The new and old sections of *Lochmonar* being joined. [*National Maritime Museum N47339*]

Two views of the new bow section for the *Lochmonar* under construction by Harland and Wolff. [*Above: George Scott collection; below: National Maritime Museum N47338*]

Cargoes and contraction

A view of the service, in late August 1934 with cargo scarce, saw seven ships on the route, compared with eleven in 1928. Outward *Dinteldijk* had cleared from London and *Drechtdijk* was in mid-Atlantic, having sailed from Swansea on 17th August. *Lochgoil* left Punta Arenas, Costa Rica, on the 24th, bound for California. Homeward, *Damsterdijk* was discharging at Rotterdam. *Lochkatrine* was clearing the Caribbean for the Atlantic crossing to Europe, followed by *Delftdijk* which arrived at Balboa on the 27th. Lastly *Lochmonar* sailed south from Portland, Oregon, the previous day.

The lack of cargo following the world financial collapse of 1929, was in part met by collaboration. In 1933 the partners, with Furness Withy, merged some port agencies and signed a five-year pooling agreement covering their seventeen ships on the service. The disparity in numbers between the three Royal Mail and four Holland America ships was addressed by one or other of the *Nebraska* or *Messoniere* class reefer ships usually identified with the Argentine meat trade.

The variety of cargo can be illustrated by the 769 tons landed at Southampton from *Lochgoil* in February 1938. It was made up of 287 pieces lumber, 1,035 manufactured doors, 12,215 cases of apples, 300 bundles of shingles, 9,024 pigs of lead, 120 bundles of broom handles, 104 bundles of plywood, 895 cases of canned goods, 600 cases of dried fruit and 464 cases of pears.

Allied and axis casualties

There was no phoney war for Royal Mail, and before peace returned three *Loch* boats and two *Dijks* were lost, with fourteen lives. The first loss suffered by Royal Mail, *Lochgoil* hit a mine laid by *U 32* soon after sailing from

Top: *Lochavon* in the Mersey. *[J. and M. Clarkson]*

Middle: *Lochmonar* in war paint at Halifax in June 1943. *[National Maritime Museum P23240]*

Bottom: of the ships which Holland America contributed to the joint service, only the *Delftdijk* came under Allied control during the Second World War. *[National Maritime Museum P22145]*

Swansea for Vancouver. Towed in and beached off the Mumbles lighthouse she was patched, refloated late in November and drydocked at Swansea. A constructive total loss she passed to the Ministry of War Transport, was towed to the Clyde in April 1940, repaired and emerged as *Empire Rowan* under Royal Mail management.

Weeks later the new *Lochavon* was commodore ship of the five ship homeward bound convoy KJF3 when torpedoed by *U 45* in mid Atlantic. Abandoned in the early hours of 14th October 1939, crew and passengers were picked up by the destroyer HMS *Ilex*. Like *Lochgoil* she was still on North Pacific service.

The next loss was in 1942. *Lochkatrine*, on ballast passage for New York in ON 115, was hit by torpedoes from U 533 early on 3rd August. Sadly nine died, 89 being picked up by the destroyer HMCS *Hamilton* and the corvette HMCS *Agassiz*. Landed at Halifax the crew were repatriated to Glasgow as distressed British seamen on board the *Strathmore*.

Only *Lochmonar* remained, and the managed *Empire Rowan*. With other Royal Mail ships they were assigned to Operation Torch, the Allied North African landings in November 1942. *Lochmonar* led a charmed life, although when she was commodore ship of one convoy, *Benalbanach* (7,153/1940) was hit and blew up. *Empire Rowan*, on her second trip, was hit by an aerial torpedo off Philippeville on 27th March 1943. Beached at Cape Collo she was a total loss. Years later, on 8th January 1951, an explosion on the wreck was attributed to unofficial salvage work by amateur divers.

Holland America also suffered heavily. When German forces invaded Holland and captured Rotterdam on 14th May 1940, three North Pacific ships were seized. All had arrived during the previous three weeks. Only *Delftdijk* remained under Allied control. She survived the war, although damaged by an aircraft attack in Flushing Roads on 10th May 1940. More seriously, another attack by German aircraft off Rattray Head on 3rd September saw her towed into Aberdeen. Patched at Leith and with cargo transhipped to *Port Dunedin*, she proceeded to the Tyne for permanent repair which took a year to complete. She sailed from the Tyne in September 1941.

Damsterdijk and *Drechtdijk* were designated as transports *RO12* and *RO13* for Operation Sealion, the German invasion of Britain. Later in 1940 *Dinteldijk* was badly damaged by fire and burnt out forward. On 23rd September 1944 she was scuttled as a blockship in the Nieuwe Waterweg, three kilometres above Maasluis. Breaking in two, her wreck was blown up in 1946 to clear the waterway. *Drechtdijk* became the German *Russelheim* in the Baltic and Norway. During the evacuation of the Eastern front she hit a mine off Swinemunde on 17th February 1945, was beached on fire and further damaged by aircraft the following month. Returned to her owners in December 1945, she was fit only to go to Ghent breakers. *Damsterdijk* served as the German *Mulhausen,* was found badly damaged at Kiel in 1945, and arrived at Rotterdam in tow on 16th February 1946. Returned to Holland America she was repaired and emerged in 1948 as *Dalerdijk.*

Post-war rebuilding

As the guns fell silent three ships returned to service. *Lochmonar, Damsterdijk* and *Delftdijk* were all in need of shipyard care for deferred wartime repairs. The first addition came in 1946 when Royal Mail bought the fast cargo ship *Empire Chieftain* which had been under their management. Renamed *Loch Ryan* she served until sold in 1960. *Damsterdijk* emerged as the *Dalerdyk* in 1948 and the following year was given a new pair of Sulzer diesels. Orders placed by Royal Mail saw two new ships launched in 1946 as the turbine-powered *Loch Garth* and *Loch Avon*. Holland America added a new ship to the service in 1950 when *Diemerdyk* was completed by Wilton-Fijenoord. She was also a turbine ship, using a set of turbines built by General Electric in 1946, possibly intended for a cancelled Victory or C3 type ship.

Lochmonar was driven ashore in a hurricane, 19th September 1948, on Little Cayman. Refloated ten days later she went to the breakers at Blyth the following year. *Delftdijk* was also damaged, hitting a mine 60 miles off Cuxhaven, outward bound from Bremen for the North Pacific, on 24th January 1950. Towed into Bremerhaven by the tugs *Danzig* and *Titan,* and then to Rotterdam by the *Zwarte Zee* (793/1933) she emerged from repairs by her builders with a new name, *Dongedyk,* more powerful MAN

Loch Avon. [Fotoflite incorporating Skyfotos]

Top: *Dalerdyk* passing through the Panama Canal. Originally the *Damsterddijk,* she was renamed after repair following the Second World War. *[Roy Fenton collection]*

Middle: *Loch Avon,* one of Royal Mail's first new postwar ships. *[George Scott collection]*

Bottom: *Loch Gowan.* A post-war fashion for long bridge decks produced some handsome cargo liners. *[Fotoflite incorporating Skyfotos]*

diesels and a new forepart. In 1958 *Loch Avon* was in the news. On 30th January she collided with the collier *Thomas Livesey* in a fogbound Thames. The collier was beached in Gravesend Reach, refloated two days later and repaired.

Three further ships were to be built for the trade. Royal Mail added the turbine *Loch Gowan* in 1954 and sister *Loch Loyal* in 1957, which had a Harland B&W diesel. Holland America commissioned *Dinteldyk* in 1957, with Pametrada steam turbines. Both the Dutch post-war ships were fitted for 60 passengers. With these settled into the service, *Loch Ryan* was sold in 1960, and renamed *Fair Ryan* for passage to Nagasaki breakers. *Loch Avon* and *Loch Garth* were sold and Furness' *Pacific Envoy* renamed *Loch Ryan* in 1967. The Furness and Royal Mail interests were being merged and this renaming helped retain the public image of the two fleets. *Loch Ryan* reverted to *Pacific Envoy* in 1970.

Royal Mail Lines' ship's movements list for 29th August 1955 gives a picture of what was probably the most prosperous period for the service, with fourteen ships maintaining the route. Apart from the *Loch, Dyk* and D-classes built for the service, Holland America had the Victory ship *Arnedyk* (7,638/1944) on the route and Royal Mail had the Liberty *Barranca* (7,253/1943) plus members of the general cargo P- and Y-classes. Outward *Dalerdyk* had sailed from London on the 17th and was in mid-Atlantic, with *Drina* (9,785/1944) due to follow any day from Antwerp. *Loch Garth* had sailed from Cristobal for the North Pacific on the 28th, five days behind *Dongedyk*. *Brittany* (5,089/1946) had berthed at Vancouver on the 25th, followed by *Pilcomayo* (5,574/1945) at Victoria on the 28th. Homeward *Loch Gowan* arrived at San Francisco on the 28th, a week after *Diemerdyk* at Los Angeles. *Duivendyk* had sailed from Cristobal on the 17th and was well out making the easterly crossing of the Atlantic, followed by the Liberty *Barranca* which was clearing the West Indies from her call at Curacao. In Europe the Victory *Arnedyk* had arrived at Liverpool, *Durango* (9,801/1944) was in port in London and *Loch Avon* at Bremen. Lastly, *Loch Ryan* was coasting from London to Liverpool.

In service *Loch Loyal* suffered engine troubles on a number of occasions. In March 1964 there was a crankcase explosion outward 800 miles south of Los Angeles, where she arrived ten days later on 20th March. A fire in her engine room on 24th October 1969 in mid-Atlantic saw

crew and passengers transferred to the *Thuringia* (10,958/1967). They were later able to return and she was towed into Ponta Delgada, from whence the tug *Elbe* (797/1959) towed her to Belfast, where she arrived for repairs on 10th November.

Run down and closure

The world was changing. The Treaty of Rome laid the foundations for a new future with Britain looking to Europe rather than the Commonwealth. In the early 1960s the effect was felt by the North Pacific Coast Line, with a fall off in cargo from the UK. With their interlinked ownership, talks between Furness Withy and Royal Mail were logical and led to rationalisation, each withdrawing two ships. But ever increasing costs on the Pacific West Coast nullified the benefits, with British Columbia longshore troubles following the British seamens' stoppage of 1966. Furness Pacific were operating a monthly sailing from Manchester and Glasgow, with Royal Mail/Holland America offering three sailings every four weeks from London and the Continent, reduced to two in 1964.

In 1965 a Furness bid for Royal Mail Lines led to full ownership, and Furness Ship Management Ltd. was formed to integrate fleets. The Furness and Royal Mail North Pacific services merged, with Holland America Line remaining a partner. Continued rationalisation saw the Manchester call close and by 1969 five Furness/Royal Mail and three Holland America ships were maintaining the service. As 1970 dawned, of the ships built for the service only *Loch Gowan, Loch Loyal, Loch Ryan* (ex *Pacific Envoy*) and *Dinteldyk* remained.

Dinteldyk arrived at Rotterdam on 2nd June 1970, completing her last North Pacific voyage, was sold and later that month became *Oriental Fantasia*. Finally 'Black Friday,' 13th November 1970, saw Furness prune loss-making areas, with the North Pacific service scheduled to close by the end of the year. Twenty three ships were listed for disposal including the last Loch, *Loch Loyal,* and the remaining four Furness' Pacific ships. *Loch Loyal* made her last arrival at Hull on 1st February 1971, and a week later was laid up at Falmouth. The following month new owners renamed her *Aegis Loyal,* a name retained until sold to Taiwan breakers in 1974.

Dinteldijk of 1950 at San Francisco. *[Roy Fenton collection]*

Royal Mail Steam Packet Company/Royal Mail Lines Ltd.

1. LOCHKATRINE 1921-1942

ON 146228 9,419g 5,812n 11,580d (502.0) 485.4 x 62.3 x 35.8/29.6 feet.

Two Burmeister & Wain-type 8-cyl. 4SCSA oil engines by Harland and Wolff Ltd, Glasgow; 5,000 BHP, 13 knots.

5.8.1921: Launched by John Brown and Co. Ltd., Clydebank, Glasgow (Yard No. 508).

1.1922: Completed for the Royal Mail Steam Packet Co. Ltd., London as LOCHKATRINE.

1932: Owners became the Royal Mail Lines Ltd.

3.8.1942: Torpedoed by the German submarine U 533 in position 45.52 north by 46.44 west whilst on a voyage in convoy ON 115 from Liverpool to New York in ballast. Of the 64 crew, 8 gunners and 18 passengers, 8 crew and 1 passenger were lost.

2. LOCHGOIL 1922-1939

ON 146679 9,462g 5,873n 11,576d. (502.0) 485.6 x 62.3 x 35.8/29.6 feet.

Two Burmeister & Wain-type 8-cyl. 4SCSA oil engines by Harland and Wolff Ltd., Glasgow; 5,000 BHP, 13 knots.

24.8.1922: Launched by Harland and Wolff Ltd, Glasgow (Yard No. 516).

12.1922: Completed for the Royal Mail Steam Packet Co. Ltd., London as LOCHGOIL.

1932: Owners became the Royal Mail Lines Ltd.

6.10.1939: Mined 4.5 miles south west of Scarweather Light Vessel, Bristol Channel in position 51.24.30 north by 4.03 west whilst on a voyage from Newport to Vancouver with general cargo. The mine was laid by the German submarine U 32 on 17.9.1939.

7.10.1939: Beached near Mumbles Lighthouse.

28.11.1939: Towed to Swansea where she was condemned as a constructive total loss.

27.4.1940: Left Swansea in tow for Glasgow, where she arrived 30.4.1940 and was subsequently repaired.

1940: Sold to the Ministry of War Transport (Royal Mail Lines Ltd., managers), London.

1942: Renamed EMPIRE ROWAN.

27.3.1943: Torpedoed and sunk by aircraft off Philippeville in Bay of Collo, north west of Bone, in position 37.16 north by 06.54 west whilst on a voyage from Glasgow to Philippeville with 4,500 tons of coal and military stores including ammunition. Of the 63 crew and 11 gunners. 3 of the crew were lost.

8.1.1951: Wreck exploded under water, cause unknown but believed to result from unofficial salvage work by amateur divers.

3. LOCHMONAR 1923-1949

ON 147677 9,412g 5,815n (502.0) 485.6 x 62.2 x 35.5/29.6 feet.

Two Burmeister & Wain-type 8-cyl. 4SCSA oil engines by Harland and Wolff Ltd., Glasgow; 5,000 BHP, 13 knots.

8.12.1923: Launched by Harland and Wolff Ltd., Belfast (Yard No. 517).

6.1924: Completed for RMSP Meat Transports Ltd., London as LOCHMONAR.

30.11.1927: Following a steering defect, grounded on Taylor's Bank revetment, River Mersey and broke in two whilst on a voyage from Vancouver to Liverpool.

2.1928: Following salvage, aft section left under tow for Belfast.

2.8.1928: New fore part launched.

1932: Owners became the Royal Mail Lines Ltd.

19.9.1948: Grounded in hurricane near Little Cayman.

30.9.1948: Refloated by the salvage vessel CURB.

17.12.1948: Sailed for Hamburg following temporary repairs at Kingston, Jamaica.

16.1.1949: Docked at Southampton and laid up until sold for scrap to British Iron and Steel Corporation. Allocated to Hughes Bolckow Ltd.

18.4.1949: Arrived at Blyth for breaking up.

Lochkatrine. [J.K. Byass]

Lochgoil. [J. and M. Clarkson]

Lochmonar. The three sisters on this page and some of the Holland America ships had the lattice derricks for which there was a fashion during and after the First World War. *[A. Duncan]*

4. LOCHAVON 1938-1939

ON 166504 9,205g 5,703n (498.0) 477.7 x 66.3 x 30.2 feet.

Two Burmeister & Wain-type 8-cyl. 2SCDA oil engines by Harland and Wolff Ltd., Glasgow; 2,052 NHP.

3.3.1938: Launched by Harland and Wolff Ltd., Glasgow (Yard No. 999).

7.1938: Completed for the Royal Mail Lines Ltd., London as LOCHAVON.

14.10.1939: Torpedoed by the German submarine U 45 in position 50.25 north by 13.10 west whilst on a voyage in convoy KJF3 from Vancouver to Liverpool, Clyde and Southampton, with 31,000 cases dried fruit, general cargo and passengers.

The short-lived *Lochavon,* probably on trials on the Clyde in July 1938. *[A.Duncan]*

5. LOCH RYAN 1946-1960

ON 164863 9,904g 7,165n 11,696d (497.6) 475.5 x 64.4 x 40.0 feet.

Two steam turbines by Richardson, Westgarth Co. Ltd., Hartlepool, double reduction geared to a single screw.

20.5.1943: Launched by Furness Shipbuilding Co. Ltd., Haverton Hill-on-Tees (Yard No. 354).

10.1943: Completed for the Ministry of War Transport (Royal Mail Lines Ltd., managers), London as EMPIRE CHIEFTAIN.

1946: Acquired by Royal Mail Lines Ltd., London and renamed LOCH RYAN.

1960: Sold to the Argonaut Shipping and Trading Co. Ltd., London (C.Y. Tung, Hong Kong) and renamed FAIR RYAN.

2.7.1960: Arrived at Nagasaki.

8.7.1960: Delivered to breakers.

10.8.1960: Demolition due to begin.

Seen above off Gravesend in 1954, the *Loch Avon* was one of the standard fast cargo liners built during the Second World War. She had been completed as *Empire Chieftain,* below. *[National Maritime Museum N34549 and P22248]*

6. LOCH GARTH 1947-1967

ON 181629 8,617g 5,132n 10,789d 498.3 x 66.3 x 30.0 feet.

Three steam turbines by Harland and Wolff Ltd., Belfast double-reduction geared to a single screw; 11,550 SHP, 16 knots.

24.9.1946: Launched by Harland and Wolff Ltd., Belfast (Yard No. 1328).

5.1947: Completed for Royal Mail Lines Ltd., London as LOCH GARTH.

12.10.1967: Left London in tow for Tamise, Belgium.

11.1967: Breaking up commenced by Jos Boel and Sons S.A., Tamise.

7. LOCH AVON 1947-1967

ON 181706 8,617g 5,132n 10,741d 498.3 x 66.3 x 30.0 feet.

Three steam turbines by Harland and Wolff Ltd., Belfast double-reduction geared to a single screw; 11,550 SHP, 16 knots.

27.11.1946: Launched by Harland and Wolff Ltd, Belfast (Yard No. 1329).

8.1947: Completed for Royal Mail Lines Ltd., London as LOCH AVON.

1967: Sold to International Export Lines Ltd., Nassau (C.Y. Tung, Hong Kong) and renamed HONGKONG OBSERVER.

1968: Owners became Singapore Malaysia Overseas Line Ltd., Singapore (C.Y. Tung, Hong Kong).

27.5.1973: Arrived at Kaohsiung to be broken up

12.6.1973: Delivered to Lung Hsing Enterprise Co. Ltd.

27.8.1973: Work commenced.

8. LOCH GOWAN 1954-1970

ON 186087 9,718g 5549n 10,624d 502.8 x 68.3 x 30.0 feet.

Three steam turbines by Harland and Wolff Ltd., Belfast double-reduction geared to a single screw; 11,550 SHP, 16 knots.

19.1.1954: Launched by Harland and Wolff Ltd., Belfast (Yard No. 1480).

6.1954: Completed for Royal Mail Lines Ltd., London as LOCH GOWAN.

5.4.1970: Arrived at Kaohsiung from Vancouver.

20.4.1970: Demolition due to commence by Hwa Zong Steel and Iron Works Ltd.

Loch Garth [J. and M. Clarkson]

Above: *Loch Avon [Fotoflite incorporating Skyfotos]*

Below: *Loch Gowan [P.A. Vicary]*

9. LOCH LOYAL 1957-1971

ON 187700 11,035g 6,447n 11,670d 502.7 x 68.4 x 41. feet.
Two Burmeister & Wain-type 8-cyl. 2SCSA oil engines by Harland and Wolff Ltd., Belfast; 10,300 BHP, 16 knots.
9.8.1957: Launched by Harland and Wolff Ltd., Belfast (Yard No. 1562).
12.1957: Completed for Royal Mail Lines Ltd., London as LOCH LOYAL.
1971: Sold to Aeakos Compania Naviera S.A., Panama (Aegis Shipping Co. Ltd., Piraeus) and renamed AEGIS LOYAL under the Greek flag.
1971: Owners became Athamas Shipping Co. Ltd., Famagusta (Aegis Shipping Co. Ltd., Piraeus).
16.8.1974: Delivered Shanghai for breaking up by China National Metals and Minerals Import and Export Corp.

Furness, Withy and Co. Ltd.

10. PACIFIC ENVOY/LOCH RYAN 1957-1971

ON 187759 9,439g 5,572n 501.2 x 63.4 x 41.0 feet.
Geared steam turbines by Parsons Marine Turbine Co. Ltd., Wallsend-on-Tyne; 15.5 knots, 8,470 SHP, 15.5 knots.
23.10.1957: Launched by Vickers-Armstrongs (Shipbuilders) Ltd., Newcastle-upon-Tyne (Yard No. 157).
4.1958: Completed for Furness, Withy and Co. Ltd., London as PACIFIC ENVOY.
1967: Renamed LOCH RYAN.
1970: Renamed PACIFIC ENVOY.
1970: Owners became Royal Mail Lines Ltd. (Furness, Withy and Co. Ltd.), London.
1971: Sold to Amon Shipping Co. Ltd., Famagusta (Aegis Shipping Co. Ltd., Piraeus) and renamed AEGIS STRENGTH.
29.1.1974: Sailed from Singapore Roads to Whampoa.
3.2.1974: Delivered to China National Metals and Minerals Import and Export Corporation.
3.1974: Under demolition at Whampoa.

Above: *Loch Loyal,* sister to the *Loch Gowan. [J. and M. Clarkson]*
Below: Furness, Withy's *Pacific Envoy* was renamed *Loch Ryan* on transfer to the North Pacific Line. *[J. and M. Clarkson]*

Details and further photographs of the Holland America ships will appear in Record 23.

A NOTE TO PHOTOGRAPH COLLECTORS

This appeal is aimed squarely at photographic collectors who may be looking for a good home for their collections. But first a few words of reassurance. As an illustrated journal, *Record* is only possible because so many photo collectors, photographers and custodians of collections so readily help us to find the illustrations of ships which we need. Their assistance is fully acknowledged, and we trust they appreciate how they help to make this journal what it is. We hope we will not seem to be turning our backs on these worthy gentlemen if we use these pages to try to extend the Ships in Focus print collection.

Over the years of producing *Record*, we have come to realise that having access to our own sources of prints, as well as to John Clarkson's large negative collection, is absolutely invaluable. Perhaps most importantly, having our own sources also provides inspiration for features. We can quickly illustrate material that turns up shortly before press day, especially that which appears in the Putting the

Record straight column. And thirdly, it means we bother collectors and custodians only when we really need to. We are therefore making this appeal to owners of photographic collections who are considering disposing of them: let us make you an offer. We can assure you that the prints will be cherished and will be put to good use, giving pleasure to *Record* readers. We may even be able to respect your wishes for disposing of it when we too have finished with it (your editors are unlikely to prove immortal).

Naturally, we need to know about the size of the collection, and something about its content. For obvious reasons, we would be reluctant to purchase large numbers of prints from John's negatives. We would also be interested in having some idea of your collection's value, and whether you wish to sell it in its entirety or are willing to split certain sections. If you would like to explore this, please drop a line to 18 Durrington Avenue, London SW20 8NT, or an e-mail to rfenton@rfenton.demon.co.uk.

CULTURE SHOCK ON THE COAST
Ian Muir

A notion to follow grandfather's footsteps from 'blue water' on to coastal ships for a time and so gain a closer knowledge of Home Trade ports, rivers, and islands had long been in my mind. While serving on deep-sea ships I had made the usual written approach to the Superintendent Engineer of an English company who owned a large fleet of coastal vessels, but had received no answering signal by company letterhead, lamp, or flag. Foreign-going experience had given no inkling of the much greater immediacy of engagement in coastal ships which I was to find tended to require a new hand at short notice even before the well-pickled body of the former crew member was found cast hard aground on Northfleet Hope, or when a relief was needed to cover someone's brief absence to mourn the demise of a (probably imaginary) relative. Leave entitlement was meagre then.

From blue water to rock dodging
Some months later the time came to leave a ship on which I had been doing a relief turn in London's West India Docks, giving an opportunity for more immediate action. Telephoning the same company around 11.00 the Engineer Super came on straightaway and, brushing aside my preamble, asked ....

'Can you join the *Sonority* as Second right away? She's at Greenhithe, and sails at 16.30 with bagged cement for Lossiemouth.'

'Yes', I said, having no idea how. 'But what...' I continued.

'Thanks', said he. 'Good luck!'

By the time my gear was gathered and a taxi phoned the Cockney dockers were returning after lunch and I had to fight my way down the ship's side boarding ladder carrying one case at a time, making myself popular. The cabbie put on an expression as though I had asked him to fly me to Cuba, but agreed the hire when the problem was explained. Leaving West India Dock we ducked under the Thames at Rotherhithe then set out for the Garden of England, where Greenhithe proved to be anything but. Months later it was discovered that a short distance inland Kent is indeed lush and green but on that narrow coastal strip under the plume path of the many chimneys of the cement works was a whitened, wasted, lunar landscape.

Humping my gear aboard it seemed I had been drafted to the *Marie Celeste;* there didn't seem to be a soul about, and that on a ship due to sail in two hours time. Eventually by dint of trying several doors the Cook was discovered, unworriedly reading the morning's paper in the warmth of his galley.

'The Skipper's at the Office and the lads are ashore for a pint. D'you want some lunch?' he asked offhandedly in his Norfolk drawl, handing me unasked a mug of 'gunfire' - well-stewed tea having the colour and consistency of bitumen laced with tinned condensed milk, an additive invariably referred to afloat as 'connie onnie'.

'I'll show you your cabin,' he said, 'then dish you something up.'

And so he did. Syd's cooking was of the plainest but it filled holes - not least his suet duff. Had such a dish been on the menu aboard *Titanic* then, speedily stuffed in the leaks, it could have saved the ship. Aboard a mere coaster the prudent stepped carefully after enjoying it, lest the vessel's trim be upset.

Soon there was a clatter of boots on the gangway as the crew returned and I was introduced to my new Chief, the middle-aged Jack Young, from Scarborough. It was soon found this was a different world which had little overt discipline, where rank was not something flashed on gold-laced cuffs or epaulettes. In the close-knit community of a coaster with seven or eight of a crew one soon learned the habits, predilections, abilities, and shortcomings of all and made the necesssary allowances.

'Rock dodgers' and 'puddle jumpers' were ways former deep-sea shipmates had referred to such heroes and, if truth be revealed, so we proved. Those 'blue-water' experts would have gone white in an instant had they been required to take a 500 tonner up the Colne to Colchester's Hythe Quay more than a week either side of the top spring tides and had heard the ship's stern dragging along the gravel river bed while larger stones went 'clonk' off the propeller blades! Come to think of it, the trip up the Yare and through Breydon Water to Norwich would have given them food

Sonority was built in 1952 by Fellows and Co. Ltd., Great Yarmouth for F.T. Everard and Sons Ltd. and seems to have led a completely blameless life with the company. The only modification apparent between the earlier aerial view above and that in the Bristol Channel opposite was the fitting of a liferaft above the bridge sometime in the mid 1960s.

After 24 years in the Everard fleet, the ship passed to owners in Devon who renamed her *Rowancraig,* but within a year she was sold, becoming *Scandia III* in 1976 and *Almy* in 1977. She was broken up in 1986. *[Above: Fotoflite incorporating Skfotos; opposite: J. and M. Clarkson]*

for thought too. Skippers going aground at Whitlingham bend had the doubtful pleasure of living aboard, stuck on the mud at the back of beyond, until the next springs came round with the changing moon; their shame visible for miles across the flat country.

Coastal voyages

Yes, it was a different world all right, but one I would rather be in if required again to face the perils of seafaring. Looking back, it was the happiest time of my life. True, there were sometimes long hours to be worked on the coastal 24-hour-watch system of four five-hour watches and a forenoon watch from 8 to 12, but with two watch keepers alternating through the odd number of watches a change of duty came each day. Everyone thus got their turn of being shaken to turn out at an unsociable 03.00, fatigued or not. Yet few voyages in fine weather were of much more than 48 hours duration, and the tedious calls at large industrial complexes allowing no time to get ashore for a break were interspersed by sunny days and leisurely evenings at pleasant harbours like Ilfracombe, Truro, Hayle, Padstow, Looe and Penryn. When such calls carried over a weekend they were as good as a holiday.

That very first coastal voyage from the Thames to Lossiemouth on Scotland's north-east coast was followed by a voyage in ballast to Blyth, Northumberland, where we loaded Geordie coal for the householders of Teignmouth, Devon. From there it was but a short ballast trip to Dean Quarry near Falmouth, a jagged crack in the coast where outlying rocks fitted with a steel spike were used to moor with main engine running to steady the ship while the chutes made short work of loading grit for the Limmer and Trinidad Lake Asphalte Company's works in Deptford Creek back on London river. This east coast - south coast shuttle was a feature of the trade, but sometimes on finishing empty in the West Country we might be granted a break and be sent to load china clay at Par or Fowey for Continental ports like Antwerp or Ghent. In December it could be ballast to Medina Wharf in Cowes, Isle of Wight, to load sugar beet for the British Sugar Corporation's factory at Selby - seventy-five miles inland from Spurn Point at the mouth of the Humber. On one all-too-rare occasion our destination was Queen's Dock, Glasgow, with a cargo of grain to be loaded at King's Lynn. I had joined the *Formality* as Chief by then, and remember that voyage almost exactly halfway round Britain for more than just the welcome weekend at home on its conclusion.

Working our way up the East Anglian coast we took the fair-weather inshore route through Yarmouth Roads, passed the great swinging beams of Cromer light, and eventually came to anchor off the Wash to await the flood tide. I think we heaved up around 07.00 to make our way in. The channel to Lynn is shallow, tortuous, and in those days at least was buoyed in such a way that those possessed of the second sight were most likely to arrive first at the homely pub on the quayside which kept civilised hours for seafarers. Having received 'Full Ahead' on the telegraph I went on deck but could make out very little, the land being scarcely visible on the murky horizon.

Returning then to the warmth of the engine room I started odd jobs, becoming so engrossed that it was something of a shock to realise there was now a different, laboured, beat to the engine. The lubricating and scavenge oil pressures being quite normal I went round to the starboard side to have a look at the exhaust temperatures. These were higher than that they should have been, but a hand test on the cooling water overboard discharge pipe suggested all was well in that department. Since we must still have some way to go I decided on another quick look on deck and make doubly sure by sighting the engine cooling water discharge, there being no handy back-lit sightglass as on *Sonority*. Climbing up by the shortest route, the port rail was reached just aft of the bridge. The engine was still running ahead but, on looking down, the trail of bubbles from where a normal flow of cooling water was failing into the sea were not leading aft but forward! The penny still not having dropped, the horrible thought occurred, 'We're not really going astern ... ARE WE? Hearing the hurried footsteps beneath, the Skipper then leaned over the bridge wing with a sheepish expression on his face,

'S'all right Chiefie,' he said in his rich Devon burr, 'we're on the putty. I was trying to cut a corner but there wasn't enough water. It'll be along in a minute though - tide's making well - just keep her going and we'll soon climb over it!'

'Bloody navigators!', I muttered as I returned below, my entire day spoiled before properly begun. But, sure enough, minutes later a quiver ran through the ship, she curtseyed slightly, and the engine's beat and the exhaust temperatures soon returned to normal. My choler eventually followed suit, though a belief remains to this day that while running aground is one thing, being put unwittingly in charge of part of the process is quite another. Strange to relate, no mention of the event in the log is remembered, and it was not the only such puddlejump experienced. The remainder of the odyssey to Glasgow's Queen's Dock was without incident, the Skipper reckoning he would be safer taking us round the Longships he knew well rather than risk a joust with the Merry Men of Mey in the Pentland Firth.

Coal, Keadby and cooks

The weekend at home was a welcome break but, everything considered, the fun was better on the Colchester trade. The company's ships regularly traded there with cargoes of grain and house coal, but the staple was gas coal for the Gas Works beside the port's Hythe Quay. Using larger ships on the spring tides and smaller on the neaps, a carousel of coasters were kept busy throughout the year. Occasionally these cargoes were shipped at Goole but the principal loading point was Keadby, a much more obscure smudge on the chart. The said riverside resort consisted in those days of a pub, a ramshackle wharf, and not much else except the sea lock of the Stainforth and Keadby Canal leading inland to the South Yorkshire Navigation and so to Sheffield. Keadby was thus on the opposite side of the Trent from Scunthorpe steelworks, so its pellucid air and photogenic qualities may be imagined.

About the only thing of interest there were the loading arrangements, which were likely the last of their kind. What passed for a main road in those parts crossed the canal at the locks then met the quay's railway sidings at a right-angled level crossing about 150 yards from the single tippler which emptied one wagon at a time into the ship's hold. About midway between ship and

Everard evolution?

Motor ships of the same basic design of *Sonority* - with a raised quarterdeck, a two-storey bridge amidships, and masts fore and aft - can be traced back in the Everard fleet as far as the *Assiduity* built by George Brown and Co. of Greenock in 1930. Over the years, length had increased from the 135 feet of *Assiduity* to the 177 feet of *Sonority* and her sister *Severity* of 1954. It is tempting to assume that this was a case of design evolving. However, Ken Garrett, Everard's former Marine Superintendent and the historian of the Greenhithe company, points out that the *Sonority's* immediate predecessors of this type, the 169-feet *Summity* of 1939 from Greenock and *Alacrity* of 1940 from Goole (top left), the 177-feet *Austerity* of 1947 from Grangemouth (top right) and *Scarcity* of 1948 from Goole (bottom left), were superficially similar ships with the only constructional differences due to individual yard's practices rather than to technological advances. Indeed, in some features the ships were decidedly anachronistic, especially the rod-and-chain steering gear with lignum vitae blocks and wedges for the rudder post.

Ken believes the *Sonority* and *Severity* had a slightly different lineage. Early in the Second World War, Reg Stanley - naval architect at Fellows' yard - had drawn up plans for three 174-foot motor coasters, plans drawn up presumably at Everards' request. The plans were endorsed with yard numbers 101, 192 and 193, but no yards are mentioned. No ship was completed to these designs, but at least one was started, at Everards' yard at Greenhithe where it was given the notional yard number 101. Steel cut by Fellows at Great Yarmouth was used, but only one shipwright and an apprentice were allocated to the work, and it was abandoned after the keel and bottom plates had been put in place and some frames had been erected. It may have been a scheme to ensure that Everards received an allocation of steel in the rather difficult times during and just after the war. Detective work by Ken Garrett suggests that the yard numbers 192 and 193 were in the sequence of the Yarmouth yard of Crabtree (1931) Ltd., in which Everard's had a strong financial interest.

The plans were very similar to those for the Fellows-built *Sonority* and *Severity*, yard numbers 356 and 357, which were also designed by Reg Stanley (reproduced left). Ken notes that these two took a long time to build (*Severity* was not completed until 1954, five years after *Sonority*), and recalls that an engineer interviewed for a job at Greenhithe claimed to have spent his entire apprenticeship at Yarmouth building the *Severity*.

Severity is shown bottom right (opposite). Both she and *Sonority* had 5-cylinder two-stroke 'O' type oil engine built by the Everard-owned Newbury Diesel Co. Ltd.

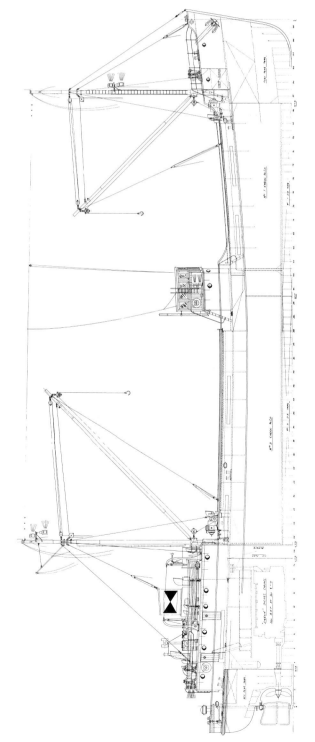

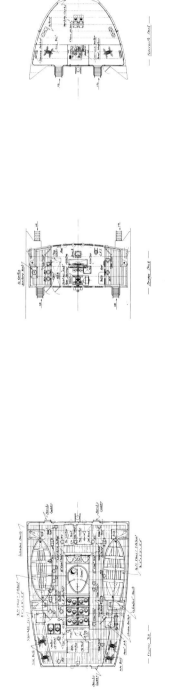

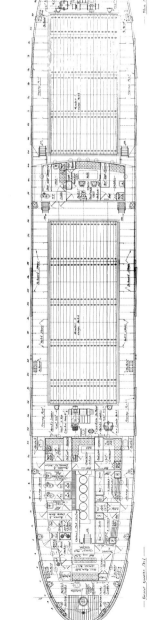

crossing was sited a wood and corrugated-iron shack containing a coal-fired vertical boiler which supplied steam to a capstan mounted at ground level. When loading was to commence the crossing gates would be set for rail traffic and a number of laden wagons detached from the train which had been shunted up to the gates by locomotive. The hook on the end of a long traveller rope was then attached to the frame of the first wagon by the shunter and several loose turns adeptly thrown round the vertical warp end of the steadily-turning capstan by his mate. At a signal from the former these were tightened and the short train drawn slowly across the road crossing into the quay yard, stopping at a turntable at the foot of an incline leading to the tippler, where the brakes of the last wagon were pinned down. Uncoupling the first wagon and using the rope round a snatch-block one wagon at time was turned if necessary, then drawn up the slight incline to the tippler which shot the contents out the wagon's end door into the ship's hold beneath. Returned to the rails, the wagon then ran down the incline to a set of points diverting it to a level lye from where the recoupled group were returned later to the main line siding for marshalling into a train.

In those days the cooking on most coasters was still done on a coal-fired cast-iron 'Trawler' stove, having a single oven to one side of the firegrate on smaller versions, and a flanking pair where larger crews were catered for. Simple seafarers constantly marvelled how, just as a ton of coal was going to have to be ordered to fill the galley bunker at the next port, the ship was sent to load a coal cargo. What could be in shipowners' minds at such times? One thing was certain, if the deck spillage that went down the galley bunker hatch happened to be of Keadby coal then some amusement could be guaranteed - particularly if a new unworldly cook had joined since the last fill of this free, fun-filled, fuel.

On our 400-ton wartime-built *Formality* the domestic wash water and the accommodation radiator circuit were heated by a coal-burning 'Britannia' boiler, a double-skinned cast iron affair about six-feet high having a firegrate within perhaps 20 inches square. This was hand stoked by a small shovel through a heavy vertically-hinged firedoor at about waist height, the retaining catch for which was broken - perhaps intentionally. This may seem to have been dangerous but in fact was not since the weight of the door and friction of the hinges kept it shut no matter how the ship jumped around in a seaway. But longer-serving crew members knew that, given the right fuel, it could be made to open by itself... When alongside at Keadby one day I heard the sailors tipping bags of deck-spillage sweepings into the bunker which had been quite empty. Analysing the distant clatter with an engineer's ear it was plain no-one had thought to close the fall-plate to prevent the small clean coal spilling out and filling the galley as well. Making my way there, sure enough, a great scatter lay about the quarry-tiled deck. So, after dropping the plate, where was the unwanted pile on the deck to go?

The heating boiler being beside the bunker, its firedoor was opened to have a look. Inside was a bright fire showing no flame, being well burned down and incandescent all over. Noting that the new cook was busy in the adjacent pantry but unlikely to be there long since lunch was almost ready for serving, I fell prey to devious thoughts. Pitching the boiler furnace with the deck spillage until there was just enough covering to black out the fire and, noting with satisfaction the heavy fumes given off at once owing to the great heat beneath, I closed the door and made an escape. Joining Skipper Cox, Ken the Mate, and Malky the Second in the saloon and giving them the wink, I took my seat beneath the duplex-burner paraffin lamp to await results. They were not long in coming.

'Wooompf!' 'Clang!' 'Aaaaarrrgh!', went the flue-full of gas, the firehole door, and the agonised cook, all in quick succession.

'You havin problems Cookie - was that the steak pie explodin?' shouted the Skipper down the short thwartships alleyway.

The Cook appeared, wide-eyed, terror struck, and gibbering; attempting to find words to tell us the length and colour of the flame that had shot out suddenly and almost singed his backside just as he bent down to open the oven. We had a hard job keeping faces straight as the Skipper said,

'You'd best watch how you fire that Keadby coal - the Chief'll show you how to get the best results.'

He needed very little further instruction.

The Empire F types were some of the most distinctive vessels on the coast in the 1950s, with their uncompromisingly angular hulls – particularly well seen in the photograph of *Hullgate*, left – designed so that each could be built in 28 units prefabricated inland and delivered to shipyards to be welded together. The design originated as a class of coastal tanker, the 'Chants', intended to carry fuel and water for the invasion of France, but it was realised that the 68 ordered were more than were needed, so 25 hulls were completed as dry cargo vessels by yards at Goole and Hessle. The photograph of *Empire Facility*, opposite page top, taken on 7th October 1945, shows how the Empire Fs looked when built, with a gun tub amidships.

The middle photograph opposite shows one of the most celebrated and longest-lived of the class, Captain JHK Griffin's *Farringay*, built at Goole as *Empire Farringay*, and subject to a great deal of rebuilding over the years. Her maindeck had been raised to improve her carrying capacity, and engines were added seemingly without the old ones being removed, until she had three, each driving its own screw. Known as the 'Black Pig' because of her paint scheme, *Farringay* lasted under the British flag until 1979 when she was sold to owners in Panama to become *Claire*.

Everards had easily the biggest fleet of Empire F-types: *Festivity, Fixity, Firmity, Flexity, Fluidity, Formality Fortunity, Frivolity,* and *Futurity*. Eight were bought from the Ministry of Transport in 1946, with the *Fortunity* arriving in 1953 from other owners.

The *Formality,* seen at the bottom of the page opposite, was completed at Goole as *Empire Favourite*. She was propelled by a seven-cylinder, naturally-aspirated, four-stroke Lister-Blackstone diesel running on gas oil. A basic, wartime-built vessel, she did not have the fuel-purifying equipment as on *Sonority* to allow the use of cheaper MDO. Ian Muir recalls that the Lister-Blackstone was unusual in that the inlet and exhaust valves were on the port and starboard sides of the cylinder heads, respectively, with their stems horizontal. Pistons were serviced by removing the marine-pattern big-end bearing then lowering the remaining assembly into the crankpit prior to removal via the port crankcase doors. Getting it all back took longer!

Everard's Empire Fs began to be sold for scrap in 1960 when it was felt too expensive to put them through their third special surveys. *Formality* was laid up in 1961 and first sold to T.W. Ward Ltd., but resold to Dutch breakers who demolished her at Krimpen-aan-der-Ijssel in August 1962. [David Hocquard; Flor van Otterdyk, J. and M. Clarkson]

FROM Z TO Z
A SELECTION OF TURNER, BRIGHTMAN SHIPS

There were so many tramp fleets under the Red Ensign during the last two decades of the nineteenth century that, after raising the capital, the promoters' biggest problem must have been finding a distinctive naming scheme. When London-based sailing-ship owner Charles J. Brightman and his partner William H. Turner took delivery of their first steamer from Sunderland in 1872 they named her *Zeus* and founded a fleet which, over the next 70 years, was to total around 30 ships (almost half of which are shown here), all but one of whose names began with the letter Z. In all they employed 25 different names, varying from the sublime to the really boring, *Zone* and *Zero* in particular obviously being products of a Friday afternoon in the ship-naming department.

Part of Turner, Brightman's fleet was engaged in the usual tramp trades, to the Mediterranean with coal then to the Black Sea for grain home, or out to South America with coal and loading grain or sometimes guano for home. Timber from the Baltic or White Sea was another regular cargo. However, as early as the *Zenobia* (2,069/1881) a number of ships were fitted with Haslam's refrigerating machinery. These reefers were fixed on long-term charter to the River Plate Fresh Meat Co. Ltd., and Mrs. Drabble, wife of the Deputy Chairman, launched the *Zone* (3,914/1903). Ships were also chartered to Houlders, for whom the second *Zoe* (2,255/1889) brought back from the Plate a cargo of frozen meat on her maiden voyage.

Until 1912 most of the fleet's ships are listed in 'Lloyd's Register' and the 'Mercantile Navy List' as owned by the two partners. William Turner and Charles Brightman would initially finance the ships, jointly taking 64 shares. As quickly as possible, shares were sold to investors, usually in small numbers, leaving the partners with only a minority of shares. William H. Turner died in February 1897, from when the Brightman family dominated the management. The surviving original partner, Charles J. Brightman died on 15th August 1917 and was succeeded by his son, Charles E. Brightman (not much inspiration shown by the child-naming department, either) who was clearly already involved in the business, as he had been elected Chairman of the Chamber of Shipping in 1909.

The 64-share method of ownership was a somewhat ponderous one, and fell into disuse as the sophistication, size and price of steamers grew, so that even one share represented a substantial investment. The *Zermatt* of 1907 was probably Turner, Brightman's first to be owned by a single-ship company. Most such companies expired when its ship was sold or lost, but the Zinal Steamship Co. Ltd. registered in 1912, initially owning just the *Zinal* (4,037/1912), went on to own other ships. After 1926 the much-depleted fleet was entirely owned by the Zinal Steamship Co. Ltd. or the newly-formed Z Steamship Co. Ltd. Shares in the companies were by then predominantly in the hands of the Brightman family. By 1940, Cecil F. Brightman, presumably a younger son or grandson of the founder, was one of the two directors.

Turner, Brightman's colour scheme was notable. The original flag and funnel were relatively simple, but late in the nineteenth century a new and quite elaborate flag was adopted, followed by new funnel colours, all giving reminders of the Z nomenclature. Very unusually, different funnel colours were used to distinguish the refrigerator ships and tramps. Many of their hulls were grey at a time when this was rare for British ships, and not just those of the reefers but also the tramps. Photographs reproduced here show that at one time the lower part of the masts were painted white with black above.

The fleet never fully recovered from its crippling losses during the First World War, its size hovering around four ships throughout the 1920s and 1930s. The last three ships were to be Second World War losses, and by 1943 the owned fleet was extinct. Management of the *Fort Buffalo* (7,133/1943) for the Government continued until 1945, but the company was not disposed to buy this or any other ships and simply faded away when the Fort's management ended.

Neither the compiler of this feature nor previous writers have found much to say about Turner, Brightman beyond the careers of its individual ships, and - in the spirit of putting history on record - we would very much welcome any further information on the company and on the owning families. Of particular interest is the early fitting of refrigerating machinery to ships for charter, and Turner, Brightman's links with the River Plate Fresh Meat Co. Ltd. and with Houlders.

The first flag and funnel recorded for Turner, Brightman. The letters on the flag are white on red.

The second, much more elaborate flag seems to have co-existed with the black funnel for a time. The four letter Zs are red on blue, the outline diamond is red, and in the central monogram the T is blue, the B red and the C white.

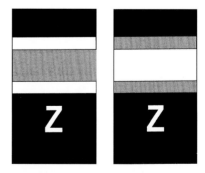

These striking funnel colours appear to have been adopted between 1895 and 1898. Indeed, the trials photograph of *Zingara* on page 87 may show an early version, quickly amended, with the letter Z above the bands. Tramps carried the funnel with the broad white band between two red bands, refrigerated ships used the version with a broad white band between two red bands. Other owners have occasionally used different basic funnel colours to distinguish tramps and reefers, but Turner, Brightman's reversal of colours may well be unique. *[J.L. Loughran]*

ZEPHYRUS (above)
Thomas Turnbull and Son; 1883, 1,351gt, 286 feet
C. 2-cyl. by Blair and Co. Ltd., Stockton
Named after the Greek god of the west wind, the iron steamer *Zephyrus* was from a well-known early iron shipbuilding yard at Whitby, a town where both building and ownership of steam tramps flourished but which quickly lost out to the Tyne and Wear.

Zephyrus was sold in 1913 and renamed *Chase Manor* for the Chasehill Steamship Co. Ltd., the first shipowning company set up by Kaye, Son and Co. Ltd. This sale is another intriguing link with the River Plate Fresh Meat Co. Ltd., as Kaye, Son and Co. Ltd. was largely concerned with managing steamers for this company, which also employed Turner, Brightman's

refrigerated ships. Whatever the reasons behind the sale, *Chase Manor* did not last long, for in 1914 she was sold to J.J. King and Sons Ltd. and broken up at Garston. This was an early site for breaking up iron and later steel ships, and the Mersey port continued to see occasional shipbreaking activity right through the twentieth century. *[J. and M. Clarkson]*

ZARATE (below)
Thomas Turnbull and Son; 1887, 2,198gt, 301 feet
T. 3-cyl. by Blair and Co. Ltd., Stockton
This photograph of *Zarate* is interesting on two counts. Firstly, it is the only one found in which a Turner, Brightman ship is wearing the funnel colours of a charterer - in this case Houlder Brothers - although their

refrigerator ships like *Zarate* presumably spent most of their lives on charter. The second point of interest is the location of the dry dock. David Hodge of the National Maritime Museum has tried hard to locate it, even tracing *Zarate's* movements for several years. She was dry docked at Newport in October 1888, but David does not think this is Newport. A liferaft visible in the original seems to read 'Eastern Dry Dock Company'. Readers' help in finding the location is eagerly sought.

On 23rd April 1900 *Zarate* was off Finisterre when the cargo of coal she was carrying from Cardiff to Rio Plata caught fire, destroying the ship. *[National Maritime Museum 9056/13]*

ZODIAC (above)
J.L. Thompson and Sons Ltd., Sunderland;
1893, 2,918gt, 312 feet
T. 3-cyl. by J. Dickinson, Sunderland
According to the message on the back of the postcard, this shot of *Zodiac* was taken as she was inbound on the Humber in the summer of 1904. From Hull *Zodiac* sailed for Tyne Dock, probably to load a coal cargo. Note the paddle tug in attendance.

In a fleet which tended to keep its ships, *Zodiac* was an early sale, passing in 1905 to Greek owner M.A. Embiricos who renamed her, perhaps surprisingly, *Gladstone*. A further sale in 1907 saw her take the more fitting name *Miaoulis*. As this she was captured and sunk by the submarine *UB 43* in the Mediterranean on 24th February 1917, on a voyage from Alexandria and Oran to Hull. *[Kevin O'Donoghue collection]*

ZYLPHA (below)
J.L. Thompson and Sons Ltd., Sunderland;
1894, 2,918gt, 312 feet
T. 3-cyl. by Blair and Co. Ltd., Stockton
In September 1915, *Zylpha* was requisitioned by the Admiralty to be employed as a submarine decoy, otherwise known as a Q-ship. She was unusually large for this role, as most Q-ships were small vessels - too insignificant, it was reckoned, for a U-boat to waste a valuable torpedo on, and which would attack with gunfire, giving an opportunity for the Q-ship to unconceal its armament and sink the submarine. Bigger ships did, however, make steadier gun platforms, and this tempted the Admiralty into forgetting the original idea, and using several larger tramps as decoys.

Zylpha, or *Q6* as she was coded, may have paid the price of this muddled thinking by their Lordships. On 11th June 1917 she was attacked by *U 82* which did not hesitate to use a torpedo on such a valuable target. *Zylpha* was north west of Fastnet at the time, and although taken in tow by HMS *Daffodil* the next day she sank off Bolus Head, County Kerry despite the buoyant cargo she habitually carried. *[Kevin O'Donoghue collection]*

ZERO (top)
J.L. Thompson and Sons Ltd., Sunderland;
1896, 3,066gt, 320 feet
T. 3-cyl. by Blair and Co. Ltd., Stockton
Appropriately, the name *Zero* was bestowed
on a refrigerated ship. This Barnard and
Straker postcard shows her on the Humber
and, from evidence of the postcards
reproduced here, the ships were frequent
visitors to Hull. There she probably met
another *Zero,* one built in the same year for
Wilson Line of Hull. Note the funnel variant
used for refrigerator ships, with a red band
between two narrow white bands.

As if Turner, Brightman's war losses
were not horrific enough, they lost further
ships to marine hazards in the years
immediately following the war. On 20th April
1922 *Zero* sank following a collision with the
US steamer *Aeolus* (12,642/1899) off Cape
Polonio, Uruguay whilst on a voyage from La
Palma in Argentina to Liverpool with frozen
meat. *[Kevin O'Donoghue collection]*

ZINGARA (middle and bottom)
J.L. Thompson and Sons Ltd., Sunderland;
1898, 3,463gt, 348 feet
T. 3-cyl. by Blair and Co. Ltd., Stockton
In the photograph below - almost certainly
taken on trials, note the name pennant and
houseflag - *Zingara* wears a funnel not
otherwise recorded for Turner, Brightman, with
the letter Z above, rather than below, the band,
which appears to be all red. This may have been
an experimental application of new funnel
colours, it being subsequently decided to modify
the bands and place the Z below them. In later
photographs - including that on page 65 -
Zingara wears the conventional funnel colours.

The photograph to the right shows
the aftermath of an explosion in *Zingara's* No. 3
hold whilst she was in Barry on 5th March
1919. The dock workers are obviously
impressed at the force of the blast which has
not only blown her hatch covers off, but has
also seriously buckled the deck and bent the
hull plating outwards. The coal cargo *Zingara*
had loaded was discharged, and on 4th April
she sailed for Sunderland for repairs, not
returning to service until August. David Hodge
of the National Maritime Museum, who very
kindly researched the photograph, has
identified the ship alongside as Heyn's
recently-built *Dunaff Head* (5,877/1918) and the
one ahead as *Antar* (3,584/1906), on which gun
mountings (but not guns) are visible.

Zingara was given an Italian name
meaning gipsy, and she certainly led a roving
life. Turner, Brightman sold her to French
owners in 1927, and she subsequently carried
the names *Djena, Lana,* and *Bona.* When
France was overrun in June 1940, she was

taken by the Germans at Rouen. There is some
doubt about the exact fate of *Bona.* During
1943, she was bombed and damaged by Allied
aircraft either at Rouen or at Le Havre. She
certainly arrived at Le Havre under tow in

September, where she was either scuttled or,
according to official German sources, broken
up. *[National Maritime Museum P27538 and
Ivor Rooke collection]*

ZULEIKA (above)

J.L. Thompson and Sons Ltd., Sunderland; 1899, 3,608gt, 348 feet
T. 3-cyl. by Blair and Co. Ltd., Stockton
In this trials view of the refrigerator ship *Zuleika,* note the walkways across the well decks and the substantial steam pipe behind the funnel. *Zuleika* survived the First World War only to be wrecked off Las Palmas on 8th October 1920 whilst on a voyage from Campana to London with meat and general cargo. *[Ivor Rooke collection]*

ZILLAH (below)

Bartram and Sons Sunderland; 1900, 3,779gt, 340 feet
T. 3-cyl. by Blair and Co. Ltd., Stockton-on-Tees
The name *Zillah* is perhaps more familiar from its use by Liverpool-based coaster owner William Savage. He gave the name to two of his small, coal- and stone-carrying steamers and to his shipowning company which was eventually bought by Coast Lines Ltd. (see Fenton RS, *Mersey Rovers*). In Savage's case inspiration came from a pet name for his wife Priscilla. Turner, Brightman may also have been thinking of a

lady, but perhaps they were just trawling through their Oxford Dictionary once again when they came across a name used for an administrative district in India.

Of the 14 ships in the Turner, Brightman fleet in 1914, no fewer than 10 were to be torpedoed or mined during the forthcoming conflict. Amongst the casualties was the *Zillah,* torpedoed and sunk by *U 46* on 22nd September 1917 north east of Kildin Island in the White Sea whilst bringing a cargo of timber out of Archangel, and bound for Lerwick. A total of 18 members of the crew were lost. *[J. and M. Clarkson]*

Zoroaster entering Mode Wheel Lock

ZOROASTER (above)
Bartram and Sons Sunderland; 1900, 3,803gt, 340 feet
T. 3-cyl. by Dickinson and Sons Ltd., Sunderland
Inbound, a well-laden *Zoroaster* approaches Mode Wheel, the last of the locks on the Manchester Ship Canal. Note her houseflag, well displayed thanks to the Salford (or was it sulphured?) wind. *Zoroaster* was, dimensionally, a sister to *Zillah,* and shared her fate as a war loss. On 29th December 1916 she was bound from the Tyne to St. Nazaire with a cargo of coal - an unusually short voyage for a ship of her size - when she hit a mine near the Sunk Light Vessel in the mouth of the Thames. The mine, laid by *UC 11,* sank *Zoroaster* with the loss of three members of her crew. *[Kevin O'Donoghue collection]*

ZAMBESI (below)
Bartram and Sons Sunderland; 1901, 3,727gt, 360 feet
T. 3-cyl. by J. Dickinson and Sons Ltd., Sunderland
Turner, Brightman's second loss during the First World War, *Zambesi* was torpedoed and sunk north west of Alexandria by *U 26* on 1st April 1917 whilst nearing the end of her voyage from the Tyne to Port Said with coal for the Royal Navy. Three members of the crew were lost. *[J. and M. Clarkson]*

ZONE (top)

J.L. Thompson and Sons Ltd., Sunderland; 1903, 3,914gt, 360 feet
T. 3-cyl. by Blair and Co. Ltd., Stockton
Zone was a refrigerated ship and is seen here at Liverpool: note the distinctive tower in the dock estate in the background.

On 30th December 1917 she was torpedoed and sunk by U 110 not far north of St. Ives. She was enroute from Boulogne to Barry with a cargo described, unappetisingly, as frozen offal. [Kevin O'Donoghue collection]

ZAMORA (middle)

J.L. Thompson and Sons Ltd., Sunderland; 1905, 3,639gt, 347 feet
T. 3-cyl. by J. Dickinson and Sons Ltd., Sunderland
A rare survivor of the First World War, Zamora was transferred to the newly-formed 'Z' Steamship Co. Ltd. in 1925. However, she was sold in 1927 to an obscure Whitby owner, W.A. Rhodes, who renamed her Brockabeck in the ownership of the eponymous Brockabeck Steamship Co. Ltd. In 1932 she became the Keila, owned by M. Suurmann of Tallinn, and was probably fortunate to escape the traumas that were visited on Estonian ships after 1939. In 1940 she was taken over by the British Government as Linda, with management allocated to Neil and Hannah Ltd. of Leith. Return to her owners after the Second World War was delayed, probably because of a dispute with the USSR over her ownership. In 1951 she was placed under the Panama flag, still as Linda, but with ultimate ownership given as M. Suurmann, A. Elb and others. Management remained with Neil and Hannah Ltd., who clearly had a relationship with several ex-Estonian shipowners, for whom they continued to manage several old steamers into the 1950s. The Linda was delivered to breakers at Antwerp in July 1958, but then was sold on, first to German and then to Dutch breakers, and was actually broken up at Krimpen a/d Ijssel, work being completed in April 1959.

This photograph of Zamora was clearly taken at a naval anchorage: a steam picket boat is taking her bow line, and a light cruiser can be seen in the distance. Fenders are in position along the length of her hull, as if she is about to go alongside and coal a warship. [National Maritime Museum P13948]

ZENADA (opposite bottom)
William Pickersgill and Sons Ltd., Sunderland;
1919, 5,764gt, 405 feet
Richardsons, Westgarth and Co. Ltd.,
Sunderland
Acquired in 1927, *Zenada* was an unusual second-hand purchase for Turner, Brightman. She had been built for Prince Line as *Arabian Prince,* one of this company's first deliveries after the First World War. Built for Prince Line's cargo liner services, she was a 'tween-decker without refrigerating equipment, and seems a strange choice for Turner, Brightman who had hitherto concentrated on tramps and reefers. She was, perhaps, bought for a specific charter, but the plain black funnel in the photograph gives no clue. Sold in 1933, she was renamed *Nestos* by Livanos Brothers who operated her under the Greek flag. *Nestos* became one of the less well known casualties of the Mersey. On 2nd April 1941 she was wrecked on East Hoyle Bank whilst inward bound to Garston with a cargo of sulphur from New Orleans. *[J. and M. Clarkson]*

ZITELLA (above)
Burntisland Shipbuilding Co. Ltd., Burntisland;
1929, 4,254gt, 371 feet
T. 3-cyl. by David Rowan and Co. Ltd., Glasgow
Two sisters delivered from Burntisland, *Zitella* and *Zouave* had the long raised-bridge deck configuration which had long been popular with British tramp owners, but which was about to become obsolete. One is rather surprised to see such a design coming from Burntisland, a yard known for its advanced thinking.

Zitella was one of those unfortunate ships wrecked when the extinguishing of lights in wartime increased the dangers to shipping. On 6th February 1940 she went ashore about one and a half miles south of Buchanness whilst carrying a cargo of iron ore from Narvik to the Tees. *[Ivor Rooke collection]*

ZOUAVE (below)
Burntisland Shipbuilding Co. Ltd., Burntisland;
1930, 4,253gt, 371 feet
T. 3-cyl. by David Rowan and Co. Ltd., Glasgow

Named after the French light infantrymen originally recruited from a tribe in Algeria, *Zouave* was both the last Turner, Brightman ship built and the last to survive. She avoided the worst effects of the shipping depression between the wars, running to the Plate and to Australia for grain and the Mediterranean with coal, with only a short four-months' lay-up in 1933. On 17th March 1943 *Zouave* was on a long voyage from Pepel via Curacao and Halifax to the Tees with a cargo of iron ore in convoy SC 122. This convoy and HX 229 which was close behind it was attacked by one of the largest groups of U-boats yet assembled, 40 boats comprising three of Donitz's 'wolf packs'. Twenty two ships were lost from the two convoys in a battle which probably represented the peak of the success for the U-boat force, the *Zouave* being torpedoed and sunk by *U 305* with the loss of 13 of the 43 crew and gunners. *[J. and M. Clarkson]*

BY BERGEN LINE FROM NEWCASTLE Part 1
Anthony Cooke

For many years, the Bergen Line was one of the most highly regarded shipping companies on the North Sea. The Bergen boats were acknowledged to be sturdy, well-built and well-maintained - as, indeed, they needed to be when coping with the rough conditions they often met. Despite their somewhat severe livery, many of the passenger ships had a certain elegance. Those black funnels, with the three thin and widely-spaced white bands, and the black hulls, with a small gold star at the bow and the rims of the portholes picked out in white, could look tremendously smart.

Services develop

Det Bergenske Damps-kibsselskab (The Bergen Steamship Company) had been formed by local merchants in 1851. Initially, its main trade was on the important route from western Norway to Hamburg; but as time went on it became increasingly involved in the routes along the Norwegian coast to the north. In particular, in 1894 it became one of the participants in the state-subsidised *Hurtigrute* (express service), which had been established the previous year by the Vesterålens Dampskibssel-skab. This vital link to the remote communities of the far north persists in modified form to this day, although much of the domestic passenger traffic now goes by road or by air and, alas, Bergen Line ships are no longer involved. For the tourist, though, the *Hurtigrute* is still a wonderful way of seeing the magnificence of the Norwegian west coast.

Over the years, the Bergen company also developed other, more far-flung services - to Rotterdam and to Iceland, for instance. It also became a partner in the Norwegian South America Line, in the County Line to Canada and in services to the Baltic ports. After the Second World War, it participated in the Scandinavian West Africa Line. But in Britain it was best-known for the express mail, passenger and cargo service from Bergen to the Tyne, which it commenced in 1890.

This was not the first such service. A former

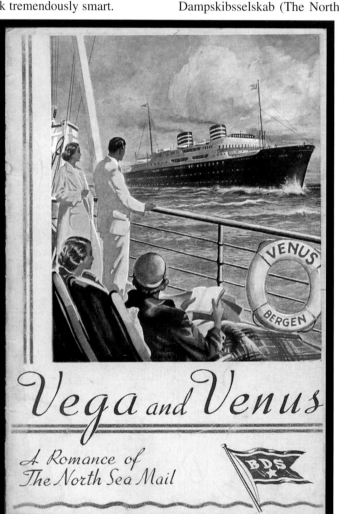

The cover of a publicity brochure produced by Bergen Line in 1938 to mark the entry into service of the *Vega*, depicted on the cover passing her running mate *Venus*. [World Ship Society collection]

Bergen Line employee, P. G. Halvorsen, had been running ships on the route since 1879. And the Bergen Line itself had for some years been carrying a few passengers on sailings from Leith, while the Wilson Line had been operating between Hull and the Norwegian west coast ports since the 1860s. For some time, Halvorsen had been seeking a mail contract from the Norwegian government, but when it was finally awarded he was forced to share it with the Bergen company and Det Nordenfjeldske Dampskibsselskab (The Northern Steamship Company) of Trondheim, further up the coast. The two newcomers were to operate a service from Trondheim and Bergen to the Tyne, while Halvorsen's ships ran out of Bergen and Stavanger. Within two years, however, his company was bankrupt. Thereafter, the Bergen and Nordenfjeldske lines ran a joint service which they advertised in Britain as the B. & N. Line and as the Norwegian Royal Mail Route.

The first ship which the Bergen Line placed in the service was the newly purchased *Mercur,* which left her home port on the 31st May 1890. She had been built at Gothenburg in 1883 as the *Kong Dag* for other Norwegian owners and was of 972 gross tons. Her compound engine gave her a service speed of 12 knots. She was, however, merely a stop-gap and remained on the Newcastle run for only a few years, although the Bergen Line kept her for use elsewhere, mainly in coastal service. In fact, built partly of iron and re-engined in 1921, she proved to be an extremely long-lived ship. (According to *Lloyd's Register* she was sold and converted into a lighter in 1939. She is believed to have been scrapped in 1952.)

The other ship with which the Bergen Line began the Tyne service was a newbuilding, the *Neptun*. A product of the Tecklenborg yard at Geestemünde, she was a 959-tonner powered by a triple-expansion engine. The following year, a further new ship arrived, the 966-ton *Mira*. She had been built by A. and J. Inglis and was notable for being fitted with electric lighting. She, too, proved to be a long-lived vessel, being retained by the company until she became a casualty of the Second World War.

'Magnificent steamers'

By international standards, the Bergen company was still, of course, a minor player. Although *Lloyd's Register* for 1892 listed a fleet of 17 vessels, they were all under 800 tons net, some as small as 200 tons.

However, the company was progressing. The *Venus* of 1893 and the *Vega* of 1895 were basically of similar design to the earlier ships, but slightly larger (1,067 and 1,164 gross tons, respectively). Fittingly, they came from yards in the north-east of England: C. S. Swan and Hunter on the Tyne and J.L. Thompson and Sons at Sunderland. They were followed by the *Irma,* larger still at 1,322 gross tons, which was completed by Sir Raylton Dixon and Co. at their Middlesbrough yard in 1905. These three latest ships maintained the Tyne service together with Nordenfjeldske's *Haakon VII* (1,347 tons, Norwegian-built, completed in 1907).

There was confusion over the name Trondheim: the Norwegian companies were still using the old-fashioned spelling, Trondhjem, while the Wilson Line preferred the German version, Drontheim. P. H. Matthiessen & Co. were a well-known Newcastle firm who had been the Bergen Line's agents on the Tyne for some years. They also acted for the Fred. Olsen Line, which ran to Christiansand and Christiania (i.e. Oslo).

'Fast magnificent Passenger and Royal Mail Steamers' they may have been, but the Bergen Line ships were still small and carried quite limited numbers of passengers. According to Dag Bakka junior, *Venus,* for instance, had a capacity on winter sailings of just 44 in first class, 14 in second and 53 in third; and in the summer, when there would be a certain amount of tourist traffic, she would carry up to 58 first, 14 second and 32 third. First class accommodation seems to have been good by the standards of the day, with some ships not only being lit by electricity but also having bathrooms.

DET BERGENSKE DAMPSKIBSSELKSKAB, BERGEN AND DET NORDENFJELDSKE DAMPSKIBSSELSKAB, TRONDHJEM.
NORWEGIAN ROYAL MAIL ROUTE TO NORWAY.

TYNE - BERGEN - STAVANGER.

The fast magnificent Passenger and Royal Mail Steamers **Irma, Haakon VII, Venus** and **Vega** are intended to leave **Newcastle-on-Tyne** (Albert Edward Dock) as undermentioned, viz:-

Every TUESDAY, 6.30 p.m......For STAVANGER, BERGEN and TRONDHJEM.
" THURSDAY, 6.30 p.m ..For STAVANGER and BERGEN.
" SATURDAY, 6.30 p.m...For STAVANGER and BERGEN.

Passengers are conveyed free by Special Train at 6 p.m. from the Newcastle Central Station, direct alongside the Steamer in Albert Edward Dock. Full particulars on application to the Agents.

P. H. MATTHIESSEN & CO., 4, Lombard Street, Newcastle-on-Tyne (Tel. Add. "MATTHIESSENS")

Above: an advertisement in a 1910 issue of *Bradshaw's General Railway and Steam Navigation Guide for Great Britain and Ireland.*

Below: the *Venus,* probably photographed soon after completion by Swan and Hunter in 1893. *[Ian Rae collection]*

Lower down the social scale, many emigrants were leaving Norway at this time. It is said, for instance, that in proportion to its population Norway sent as many migrants to the United States as did almost any other country, including Ireland. Until the opening of the Norwegian America Line in 1913, many of them travelled initially to ports on the British east coast and were then taken by rail to either Liverpool or Glasgow, where they would be loaded onto one of the Atlantic steamers sailing from those ports. The limited amount of third class capacity on the Bergen Line ships would seem to confirm, though, that much more of this traffic went via the Wilson Line ships to Hull, from where there were good rail connections to Liverpool, rather than on the Newcastle steamers.

Norway's need to import coal had been one of the main incentives behind the establishment of the early steamship services across the North Sea. By the time the Bergen Line began running on the route from the Tyne, however, most of this trade was being handled by pure freighters. It seems unlikely that the mail steamers carried any great quantity of such a dirty commodity. They did handle a variety of more general cargo, however, usually in three holds, two fore and one aft.

After the advent of the *Irma*, the service followed a settled pattern for some years. With tourist traffic growing, some summer sailings included visits to the more spectacular fjords between Bergen and Trondheim and some voyages were extended beyond the Arctic Circle as far as the North Cape. The famous visit to the Cape of the King of Siam, cruising in a private steam yacht, attracted much publicity in those royalist times and is said to have encouraged many others to make the journey.

In 1914, the company was sufficiently encouraged by prospects to order a larger steamer for the route. With a registered length of 305 feet and a tonnage of 2,625 gross, the *Jupiter* was delivered by the Lindholmens Varv of

The *Jupiter* of 1916 at North Shields. *[George Scott collection]*

Gothenburg late in 1915. With an additional deck of superstructure and carrying up to 225 passengers, she was a considerable advance on her predecessors but she did not have their good looks. Whereas the earlier passenger ships had a gracefully raked appearance, the *Jupiter* had an uncompromisingly upright profile. She was a faster ship, though, with a service speed of 15 knots and was said to be the quickest Norwegian merchant ship of the day, except only for the two transatlantic liners *Kristianiafjord* and *Bergensfjord* of the new Norwegian America Line.

By now, of course, the First World War was raging but Norway remained neutral and the Newcastle service continued, although obviously the tourist traffic had ceased. Steamers were often stopped and searched by the Royal Navy. But, as time went on, even neutral Norwegian ships with their name, country and national colours writ large along their sides were not immune from attack by German U-boats. Among those sunk was the *Vega,* which fell victim to *U 78* in November 1916. This, together with the huge cost of insurance (and of coal) forced the company to close the Newcastle service early in 1917. Some months later, the *Jupiter* was chartered to the British Government for whom she ran an emergency service between Bergen and Aberdeen under the management, rather improbably, of the Union-Castle Line. She is said to have been given some armament and to have been camouflaged with dazzle patterns. Temporarily, she was registered in London and flew the British flag.

New and second-hand ships

In 1919, with the war over and the Newcastle service running again, the company ordered a new ship which would be compatible with the *Jupiter*. Called *Leda* and delivered by Sir W.G. Armstrong, Whitworth in 1920, she was similar in many ways to her running-mate. In contrast to that ship, however, she had something of the raked elegance of the earlier Bergen Line passenger steamers. Most notably, she was the first turbine-driven passenger liner on the North Sea, being powered by two sets, double-reduction geared to a single screw. Her gross tonnage was 2,520. The ageing *Venus* was retained as the third ship in the Tyne service, with the Nordenfjeldske company withdrawing from the route in 1921 and the *Irma* becoming a more or less full-time cruise ship.

Cruising, in fact, became an important activity for the Bergen Line. In 1920, they bought the *Meteor* (3,717/1904) from the British Government. As a member of the Hamburg America Line's luxurious cruising fleet, this vessel had been well-known along the Norwegian coast before the War. With her clipper bow and tall funnel, she was modelled on the private steam yachts of royalty and the super-rich of the day. She was emphatically a first class-only vessel. Like most of the other German merchant ships which had managed to survive the War, the *Meteor* was seized by the Allies. By coincidence, she already had a 'heavenly body' name compatible with the Bergen Line's own habits of nomenclature and, so, no change was necessary when they bought her. In any case, the name *Meteor* still carried a certain prestige. She was sufficiently successful to provoke competition - in 1925, the Nordenfjeldske company acquired the former British Royal Yacht *Alexandra* and converted her into the cruise ship *Prins Olav*. (The British royals had for years been a two-yacht family, also having the more famous *Victoria and Albert*.)

Even more notable, however, was the *Stella Polaris*, which the Götaverken yard of Gothenburg delivered to the Bergen Line in 1927. Still with the appearance of a large steam yacht (although she was, in fact, a motorship), she rapidly became one of the most famous and exclusive cruise ships of the day, carrying wealthy passengers to distant parts

The *Leda* of 1920 was a near sister of *Jupiter,* but with turbines, the first in a North Sea passenger ship. Once the *Venus* arrived in 1931 she was redeployed on routes to Hamburg and Rotterdam. *[George Scott collection]*

of the world. It was the *Stella Polaris* which really established the Bergen Line's reputation as an international shipping company.

Throughout the post-First World War period, the company grew both in size and stature. *Lloyd's Register* for 1932-33 listed the fleet as 46 ships plus a further two Bergen Line freighters under the management of the Norwegian South America Line and one under the management of County Line.

Outpacing the Swedes

There were problems on the Tyne route, however. In 1929, Swedish Lloyd introduced two notable 4,000-ton turbine steamers into their service from Gothenburg to London. These were the famous Swan, Hunter-built *Suecia* and *Britannia,* which had a service speed of 17^1/$_2$ knots. It might be thought that ships sailing from Gothenburg could hardly

have posed a threat to the Bergen Line, running from the west coast of Norway. What was at stake, however, was the important passenger traffic from southern Norway. True, the Fred. Olsen Line was running from Oslo to the Tyne, but theirs was a slower service, partly because they had to make the long trek down Oslofjord before reaching the sea. Passengers for whom time was important tended to take the train from Oslo to Bergen and then join a Bergen Line ship. Now, they had another alternative - train to Gothenburg and then Swedish Lloyd to London - particularly attractive to passengers bound for the south of England. Clearly, the Bergen Line had to react.

Fortified by an improved contract from the Norwegian postal authorities, the company placed an order with the Helsingør shipyard in Denmark in August, 1929. The new liner, at 5,407 gross tons the largest on the North Sea, entered service in May 1931. She was the famous

The motor vessel *Venus* of 1931 as built. She was rebuilt - improving her appearance - after being sunk at Hamburg in 1941 and lasted until 1968. *[Author's collection]*

second *Venus* - queasy travellers might, perhaps, have preferred the term 'infamous', as she proved to be a vigorous 'roller' and was very widely known as 'the Vomiting *Venus*'. This disconcerting fault notwithstanding, she was a superb ship and became popular. For a few weeks, she was the world's fastest motor ship, achieving 20.64 knots over the measured mile during her sea trials in May 1931. (Lloyd Triestino's *Victoria* beat that record the following month.) With a service speed of 19 knots, the *Venus* could outpace the Swedes. A twin-screw ship, she was powered by two 10-cylinder Burmeister & Wain four-stroke diesels. In appearance, she was very much in the modern motorliner style, with two fairly broad funnels of medium height and a cruiser stern. She could accommodate up to 201 first class passengers and 76 second class.

Two-tiers
The service between Bergen and the Tyne now became a two-tier affair. The splendid new *Venus* left Bergen every Monday and Thursday at 11.30 am and was due to arrive at the Tyne Commission Quay 21 hours later. She sailed on the return trip at 8.00 pm every Tuesday and Saturday. The *Jupiter* - still a coal-burner, incidentally - crossed more slowly via Stavanger and charged slightly lower fares. Advertisements offered rail connections to and from Oslo, by sleeping car if desired, and mentioned that 'Norwegian State Railway coaches from Oslo run from the Station at Bergen to the Quayside in connection with the Newcastle vessels'. With admirable chutzpah, they also touted rail connections with Gothenburg and Stockholm, thus taking on Swedish Lloyd at their own game. The service was still known as the B. & N. Line, despite the fact that the Nordenfjeldske company had quit it years ago. The *Leda* had by now been transferred to the Bergen to Hamburg route.

The new ship came into service at an inauspicious time: the Great Depression was exerting its malign influence throughout the World, not least on shipping and tourism. Nevertheless, the *Venus* established herself. It was not, though, until May 1938 that the company was able to take delivery of a worthy running-mate for her. The order had been made possible by a barter deal. Some years earlier, the Mussolini government in Rome, who were eager to keep Italian shipyards in employment, had brokered a deal whereby the Poles had ordered two trans-Atlantic liners, the *Pilsudski* (1935) and the *Batory* (1936), and had paid for them mainly with shipments of coal. The order for the

Bergen Line's new *Vega* was made possible by an arrangement whereby the Norwegians sold the Italians huge quantities of stockfish.

Built at the Trieste yard of the Cantieri Riuniti dell' Adriatico, the *Vega* was an improvement on the *Venus*. At 7,287 tons gross, she was bigger - not only was she longer, but she was also slightly beamier. She was quicker, too - her twin Trieste-built Sulzer 10-cylinder engines gave her a service speed of 21 knots. Furthermore, the outstanding architect and interior designer Gustavo Pulitzer Finali was responsible for her passenger spaces. Brochures issued at the time shew that, while a few of her public rooms had a surprisingly traditional look, most of them were in the modern, clean-lined *novecento* style for which he was famous. Accommodation was provided for 217 first class passengers and 248 second. Clearly, the *Vega* was a very high-class ship indeed.

Destruction and reconstruction
Unfortunately, she had little time to make her mark. When the Second World War erupted in September 1939, she and the *Venus* were laid up. Although Norway was once again neutral, the risks were too high and the cost of insurance became impossible. The *Jupiter* and the *Leda* were also withdrawn and it was left to the small, 48-year old *Mira* to maintain the link with the Tyne. On 5th April 1940 she was attacked by a German bomber but survived. In any case, however, the German invasion of Norway three days later brought down the curtain.

Like so many other companies, the Bergen Line suffered badly during the war. Many of the passenger ships were requisitioned by the Germans and were lost. Of the vessels which had seen service on the Tyne route, the *Mira*, the *Irma*, the *Leda,* the *Venus* and the *Vega* were all sunk. After the war, the *Leda* and the *Venus* were raised - the former was beyond repair but it proved possible to rebuild the latter. The *Vega* had been largely burnt out but her engines could be salvaged and were eventually installed in two tankers. The *Jupiter* came through, relatively unscathed.

Even while Norway was under Nazi occupation, however, the directors of the Bergen Line had been planning ahead. Clearly, rebuilding the fleet would not be easy in the conditions likely to prevail after the war. Early in 1944 they reached a secret understanding with the Svea company of Stockholm whereby the Swedish line would purchase the 3,190 ton motorship *Astrea*, which was on the market, and

The Finnish-built *Astrea* was something of a stop-gap on the Newcastle service, but after transfer in 1953 she sailed on Bergen Line's Rotterdam route until 1966. *[George Scott collection]*

would sell her on to the Bergen company when peace was restored. The *Astrea* had been ordered before the war by Finska Ångfartygs A/B (the Finnish Line) for their well-known cargo and passenger service between Turku and Hull. She was completed by the Crichton-Vulkan yard at Turku in 1941, by which time, of course, the service had been closed down. Damaged by bombing, she was laid up. In 1944, Svea took delivery of her and sent her to their associated company, the Finnboda shipyard in Stockholm, who refitted her with rather more passenger accommodation (138 berths, against the original 50). Very obviously, however, she was still primarily a cargo ship. With her split superstructure and typical Finnish Line rim-topped funnel, the *Astrea* must have seemed something of an alien in the Bergen fleet. The little *Lyra* (1,475/1912), which before the war had maintained the Iceland route, re-opened the Tyne service as early as July 1945 and the *Astrea* joined her in September. The *Astrea* remained one of the mainstays until more suitable tonnage became available in 1953, when she was transferred to the Bergen to Rotterdam route.

In March 1946, the situation improved enormously when the *Jupiter* came on to the Tyne route. She had been lying at Copenhagen when the Nazi forces in Denmark surrendered in March 1945 and she was handed back to her owners, intact but in sore need of refurbishment. However, it was the triumphant return of the *Venus* in May 1948 which restored the service to something approaching its pre-war standard. She had been sunk by Allied bombers in April 1945 while acting as a submarine depot ship in Hamburg. The forward part of her hull had been shattered but she was raised and towed to her birthplace at Helsingør, where she was rebuilt. She was given a new bow - higher, a little longer and with a modern rake. Her superstructure was remodelled and, always an impressive ship, she now became a good-looking one. Her gross tonnage had increased from 5,407 to 6,269. In the winter months, when passenger traffic on the North Sea was slack, she was used in a successful new service from Plymouth (later Southampton) to Madeira.

Vega: patronage and embarrassment

Norway's shortage of foreign currency meant that it was some time before a replacement for the lost *Vega* could be contemplated. Eventually, in 1951, an order was placed with Swan, Hunter and Wigham Richardson. The

importance of the new ship, the second *Leda*, was recognised by royal patronage. She was launched on the 3rd September 1952 by Princess Astrid, who was accompanied by her father, Crown Prince Olav. Then, in April 1953, King Haakon was on board for a celebratory cruise along Oslofjord. Unfortunately, the *Leda* ran aground - the embarrassing plight of this intruder from Bergen must have caused wry amusement in the Oslo shipping community.

Once in service, however, the *Leda* proved to be immensely popular and successful. A 6,670-tonner, with an overall length of 436 ft. 8ins., she was a very modern ship. She was, for instance, the first Norwegian vessel to have fin stabilisers (they were fitted to the *Venus* shortly afterwards) and her superstructure was largely built of aluminium. Cargo handling was by cranes rather than derricks. Perhaps surprisingly, in view of the success of the motorships *Venus* and *Vega,* she was driven by Parsons' turbines. She proved to be smooth running and fast, with a service speed of 22 knots. In 1954, she set a record by crossing from the Tyne to Stavanger in 16 hours 27 minutes, reaching Bergen two hours later.

In appearance, she was very much in the latest fashion, as exemplified by such contemporary liners as the *Caronia, Augustus* and *Giulio Cesare* - raked bow, signal mast abaft the bridge, imposingly broad funnel, cruiser stern. There was one further innovation: she was almost certainly the first major passenger ship to offer cafeteria-style catering. The Bergen company had obviously decided that times had changed and that they must encourage less affluent travellers to cross the North Sea. Accordingly, the *Leda* could accommodate 384 in tourist class, as against just 119 in first, and a single tourist class fare of £7 was announced, with passengers buying their own food in the cafeteria. First-class passengers continued to enjoy the traditional style of service, of course. At the time of the *Leda's* debut, a story circulated which was probably apocryphal but is worth repeating. It was said that the panelling in her first class observation lounge was made from Cuban mahogany which had been found in some remote corner of the shipyard, wrapped in newspapers dated 1907, the year Swan, Hunters completed their greatest ship, the *Mauretania.* Was the *Leda's* panelling made from wood left over from that famous record-breaker?

Leda at Bergen, soon after her completion in 1953, with the rebuilt *Venus* ahead of her. *[Ian Rae collection]*

A new cruise ship

In addition to this investment in tonnage for the Tyne route, the Bergen company had spent heavily on freighters and on new passenger/cargo vessels for the *Hurtigrute*. It was from the design for two of the latter that a further passenger ship evolved. The famous cruising yacht *Stella Polaris* had survived the war and had been restored and returned to service. But many of her rich, leisured passengers either no longer existed or had ceased to be so wealthy. Furthermore, newer ships were now offering more modern facilities. In 1951, therefore, the *Stella Polaris* was sold. But the Bergen Line had no intention of quitting the cruise business altogether. Already, they were offering the *Venus's* wintertime sailings to Madeira as moderately-priced round-trip cruises. Now, in 1955, they introduced a multi-purpose vessel which not only acted as a reserve for the North Sea and *Hurtigrute* services, but could also be easily converted into a single-class cruise ship. A slightly larger, slightly more powerful version of the *Hurtigrute* design, the new vessel came from the same Danish yard, the Aalborg Vaerft. Reviving the famous name *Meteor,* she was a single screw motorship of 2,856 gross tons. She looked foursquare and purposeful rather than elegant but wore a cruising livery of white hull and buff, rather than black, funnel - still with the famous three white bands, however. By closing off some of her less desirable cabins and by sliding a few partitions, the *Meteor* could be quickly converted from a two-class short sea and coastal liner into a comfortable, if not overly spacious, small cruise ship carrying up to 160 single-class passengers.

She made her cruising debut earlier than anticipated when, in March 1955, the *Venus* was blown seriously aground while battling with gale force winds in Plymouth Sound. It was several days before she could be refloated in a badly damaged state and the *Meteor* was hurriedly brought in to complete her schedule of voyages to Madeira. That done, she appeared briefly on the Tyne service before starting her own cruising programme. In fact, she was not used very much on the North Sea routes and after 1958 she became a rather successful full-time cruise ship. In 1970,

she was sold to a new company called Meteor Cruises, which the Bergen Line set up jointly with another local shipowner, Rolf Wigand. On the 22nd May 1971, a horrific fire broke out in her crew accommodation while she was cruising off the coast of Alaska. Thirty two crew members were trapped and died. The *Meteor* remained afloat and, shepherded by Coast Guard vessels, she eventually made her way to Vancouver, listing but under her own power. She never sailed for the Norwegians again, being sold to the Epirotiki Line of Piraeus, who had her restored as the *Neptune.* She had a long career and it was not until February 2002 that she went for scrapping at Aliaga.

The age of the car

By the early 'sixties, in the new motor age, many passengers expected to be able to take their cars with them when they crossed the North Sea. Both the *Venus* and the *Leda* had garages, but for only 30 or 40 vehicles, which were loaded on board by crane. It was a time-consuming business, and a worrying one for nervous owners who disliked seeing their cherished cars dangling precariously in mid-air. The *Venus* would soon need replacing and the new ship would clearly have to provide drive-on facilities for a much larger number of vehicles.

The story has already been told in the article on the Fred. Olsen Line in Ships In Focus *Record* 18 of how the Bergen Line and Fred. Olsen agreed to place a joint order for a remarkably versatile new passenger/cargo/car ferry. It will be recalled that the 9,500-ton ship was delivered by the Lübecker Flender Werke in 1966 and was registered in two separate names - when running for the Bergen Line she was the *Jupiter;* when being operated by Fred. Olsen she was *Black Watch.* In the summer months, she sailed for the Bergen company on the routes to the Tyne and to Rotterdam; in winter she became a Fred. Olsen ship, operating cruises between London and the Canary Islands, from whence she returned carrying large quantities of tomatoes and other produce in cooled holds. The ingenious conversion from one rôle to the other could be accomplished in just 48 hours. Noted for the Fred. Olsen-style figurehead at her bow, her

Jupiter of 1966 introduced the radically new concept of sailing for Bergen Line in the summer as *Jupiter,* and working for joint owners Fred. Olsen Line as *Black Watch* in the winter. She is seen from South Shields on 30th July 1966. Note the yellow funnel bearing the BDS flag. *[George Scott]*

After two years' service for Olsen, the *Black Prince* of 1966 also came into the joint ownership of Bergen Line, running for the latter as *Venus* between April and October every year. *Venus* is seen passing North Shields on 28th August 1972. *[George Scott]*

bay window-shaped bridge front and her helmet-like funnel, she was an immediate success. She was, in fact, very much an Olsen ship, much of the basic design being the work of that company's very innovative technical department.

Olsens also took delivery of a virtually identical sister ship, called *Black Prince* and owned entirely by themselves. In 1968, having ordered the very similar but somewhat larger *Blenheim,* they sold a 40% share in *Black Prince* to the Bergen company under a comparable arrangement to that already covering ownership of *Jupiter/Black Watch.* Henceforth, she too had dual names - *Black Prince* and *Venus,* the famous old Bergen Line favourite of that name being sold for scrapping. Both sisters had hugely successful careers, although *Venus* was out of action for much of the summer of 1973 after striking an underwater object at Trondheim.

The *Leda* continued in service, maintaining the Tyne route single-handedly during the slack winter months, but her days were numbered. Although only 21-years old, she was withdrawn in late 1974, being temporarily replaced by charters of DFDS's *England* and *Dana Sirena* and Fred. Olsen's *Blenheim* and *Bolero.* For three years the *Leda* swung idly at anchor in Bergen harbour. The subsequent career of this fine ship makes very sad reading. Passing through the hands of a succession of owners, she served as an accommodation vessel at the Stord Vaerft shipyard and at an oil rig construction site at Stornoway in the Hebrides. She was then rebuilt as a cruise ship. Under the names *Albatros, Betsy Ross, Amalfi* and *Star of Venice,* she endured fires, mechanical breakdowns, detention for a customs offence and frequent arrests for debt. Finally, she was scrapped at Aliaga in 2001, just months before the same fate befell her former fleet mate *Meteor.*

Visions and reality

There might have been another Bergen Line passenger ship. In March, 1966, two months before the delivery of *Jupiter/Black Watch,* the company announced that they would be placing an order with Swan, Hunter and Wigham Richardson for a new vessel, intended mainly for cruising. With an estimated displacement tonnage of 7,080, she was to be 450 feet long and to have accommodation for 205 passengers. An artist's rendering of the proposed design shews a modernistic ship with a streamlined, finned funnel. As on the contemporary *Oriana, Canberra* and *Italia,* the lifeboats were to be tucked inboard on a lower deck, thus leaving an uncluttered upper deck. It was announced that the new ship would have twin screws driven by Italian-built Sulzer 10-cylinder diesels, which would give her a service speed of 19 knots. Unfortunately, the deal collapsed. Swan, Hunter had tendered a low price of about £4 million because they needed the work. By mid-April, however, they had booked orders for a ro-ro ferry and a large tanker and were no longer prepared to accept one whose profitability was doubtful. Regrettably, nothing more was ever heard of this attractive project. A further proposal, for Bergen Line participation in a ferry service between Florida and Mexico, also proved abortive.

One final passenger shipping project did get off the ground, the Royal Viking Line. In June, 1972, the Bergen company took delivery of the *Royal Viking Star,* a 21,847 gross ton cruise ship built by the Wärtsilä yard in Helsinki. With her raked and curved bow and long superstructure, she was very much in the modern mode for such vessels. Costing nearly $19 million, she had accommodation for 539 passengers. The Royal Viking Line was a joint venture between three well-known Norwegian shipping companies: the Bergen Line; their old allies, the Nordenfjeldske company; and A. F. Klaveness. Each participant contributed a single ship to the new fleet, all similar and all ordered from Wärtsilä.

Almost alone at first, Norwegian owners were reviving passenger shipping after the worldwide collapse of the old liner services following the advent of the commercial jet aeroplane. Companies such as the Royal Caribbean Cruise Line (another threesome partnership between well-known Norwegian shipowners), Flagship Cruises and the Kloster family's Norwegian Caribbean Line were among the first to foresee the huge growth of the cruise market and to have the courage to risk large sums of money in building new ships for it. Royal Viking catered for a rather wealthier, more exclusive clientele than most of the others and eventually became recognised as one of the standard-setters for the cruise industry. A large proportion of its passengers were American and, whereas many of the other lines concentrated on the Caribbean market, it offered worldwide itineraries. With fuel and other costs rocketing upwards, the seventies were not a good time to be embarking on a new shipping venture but eventually the Royal Viking Line established itself very successfully. In 1981, the *Royal Viking Star* was sent to a German shipyard to be lengthened, resulting in an increase in her passenger capacity from 539 to 758. Similar operations were carried out on her two sisters.

The end of the Bergen Line

The late 1970s and early 1980s were difficult for shipowners and, under new and more ruthless management, the Bergen company went through a painful period of retrenchment. The coastal cargo operations were merged with those of other companies to form a new concern, Nor-Cargo. The Bergen Line withdrew from participation in the *Hurtigrute,* selling its coastal passenger fleet to the Troms Fylkes Dampskibsselskap of Tromsø. The fleet of deep-sea tankers and freighters was run down. In 1984, the Bergen Line and the Nordenfjeldske company, the remaining partners in the Royal Viking Line, sold it to the Kloster group of Oslo.

Earlier, in 1975, the Bergen Line and Fred. Olsen had integrated their North Sea services and operated them under their joint names. Then, in 1981, they sold them to the expanding DFDS company of Copenhagen, who took *Black Watch/Jupiter* and *Black Prince/Venus* on charter each summer. (They both returned to Fred. Olsen for their Canary Islands service during the winters.)

As a result of these various deals, the Bergen company became less of a shipping company but accumulated reserves of cash, which made it an attractive target for a take-over bid. In November, 1984, the Anders Jahre company Kosmos gained control after a fierce battle with two well-known Norwegian industrialists, the Blystad brothers. This marked the end of the Bergen Line as an independent concern. *Venus* still spent her summers on the Newcastle route but she now ran for the Norway Line, a new Kosmos company. *Jupiter* remained under charter to DFDS, who used her on services to Denmark and Sweden.

In 1986, the arrangement between Bergen and Olsens, under which they shared ownership of the two vessels, expired. *Black Prince/Venus* now became wholly-owned by Olsens, who had her converted into a full-time cruise ship which, after an uncertain start to her new career, has been tremendously successful. *Black Watch/Jupiter* passed into the hands of the Bergen company who promptly sold her to the Norway Line. In 1988, the remnants of the Bergen Line were sold to a consortium of other Norwegian shipping concerns who proceeded to dismantle the company.

Thus, an important and greatly respected line faded away. It is still possible, though, to get a hint of the old Bergen style. One of their former *Hurtigrute* ships, the sturdy-looking *Nordstjernen* (2,194/1956), still runs summer cruises to Spitsbergen for her present owners, the Troms Fylkes company, and occasionally deputises on her old coastal route.

A fleet list and more photos will be included in Record *23.*

THE DEVELOPMENT OF OFFSHORE SUPPORT VESSELS Part 3
Peter Wynne

Supply vessels at work

The basic role of the supply vessel has not changed, despite the many developments discussed in these articles. Perhaps this is an opportune moment to consider the delivery aspect of supply vessel operations, as most ship watchers only see the vessels in port.

The rig or established platform should - to give the simplest of examples - be considered as an island with little or no natural resources. So - if you need it - you bring it with you. Thus water, oil fuel for generators, food and every little luxury - down to a bar of soap - has to be brought to the rig. Then, of course, there are all the necessities for drilling the wells.

It must be remembered that the supply vessel is only equipped to deliver the bulk cargoes - liquids and powders - all of which are pumped to the rig or platform. All other items have to be lifted off the open after deck by the cranes that are installed on the platform or rig.

To facilitate the unloading operation, the vessel carrying supplies is berthed stern-on to the rig or platform. Depending upon sea conditions, it may be possible to actually have mooring lines attached, but the vessel still must use her engines and thrusters to maintain her position. Controllable pitch propellers are of great benefit in this operation. One feature of offshore support vessels that has not been previously mentioned is the fact that almost every vessel is equipped with a bridge console or an independent control cabin that faces aft. The officer of the watch can thus control the vessel to maintain its position with ease and - most importantly - has a clear view of the entire after deck during the unloading operation.

The deck cargo, as mentioned earlier, can consist of a variety of commodities. The oil industry has developed a mini-container - basically an eight-foot cube - which is easily handleable and whose weight is within the capabilities of cranes on the rig or platform. There is also drill pipe, well casing, palletised bags of chemicals for drilling, gasses in bottle banks, spare parts and a multitude of small items. Sometimes there are even passengers. All the material has to be unloaded in the safest yet speediest manner no matter what the state of the weather. Drilling is a 24-hour operation and companies cannot afford to stop. Frequently, the open deck of a supply vessel is awash whilst the unloading operations take place. The crewmen have to know exactly when to connect the hook of the crane to the lift and the crane driver on the rig has to know when to start to hoist as the vessel pitches and rolls many metres below.

The platform supply vessel

A further development of the supply vessel is the platform supply vessel, which to all intents and purposes is a supply vessel which has been constructed with a hull that is longer than the conventional supply vessel and is thus able to carry drill pipe in double stacks on the after deck. The established platforms are able to produce their own water and power, and the platform supply vessel is therefore equipped mainly to supply bulk powders for drilling purposes, fuel and deck cargo. In recent years platform supply vessels have been built with more solid bulwarks aft as a means of keeping the working deck free of water.

The platform supply vessel is a development of the pipe carrier, which was introduced to provide the specific service that its name suggests. These vessels were built with a length to suit the double stacking of pipes and the bulwarks aft were high and the inner faces sloped as if to form hopper sides. The degree of slope varied from design to design but other vessels had open cargo rails, which had a similar sloping effect. The role of these vessels is to carry heavy pipe for the construction of pipelines that are laid on the seabed to bring the oil and gas ashore. Specialist pipe-lay barges lay these and the pipe is delivered to the lay barges in an open seaway with the pipe carrier berthed alongside. Their decks are specially strengthened as the pipes that are carried are of substantial diameters and, in almost all cases, are encased in concrete, which adds substantially to the weight of each piece of pipe.

Stirling Clyde passing under Erskine Bridge on 17th July 1996. The well-protected deck area can be seen in this view of the 1996-built platform supply vessel. She is one of a class of four 82.9 meter vessels named after Scottish rivers that was operated by Stirling Shipping Ltd. She has a deck cargo capacity of 2,700 tons. Enclosing the after deck with more substantial bulwarks offers better protection to the cargo as well as to the crew who are working on the after deck during unloading operations.

Cumbria Service is an example of an early design of platform supply vessel, built at Appledore in 1977 as *Cumbria Shore*. She was one of the 64.3 meter 'Kingdom' class operated by Offshore Marine Ltd. and has a deck cargo capacity of 744 tons. After the company was taken over by Zapata in 1980 she became *Cumbria Service*. She still carries this name, although now registered in Vanuatu, after Zapata had been swallowed up by the mighty Tidewater Marine Service conglomerate.

Far Service, built in 1995 by Soeviknes Vaerft for Farstad Shipping, is an example of a UT 745 type platform supply vessel from Ulstein. She is 83.8 meters long with a deck cargo capacity of 2,750 tons. At the time of writing, she is registered in the Isle of Man.

Safe Truck at Aberdeen on 19th July 1996. Built in 1996 by Soeviknes Vaerft for UK owners Seatruck Shipping Ltd., this platform supply vessel is a UT 755 type from Ulstein. She is 67 meters long with a deck cargo capacity of 1,550 tons.

Smit Marlin. Launched as the *Smit-Lloyd 61* in 1977, this platform supply vessel has had various names and now operates as the *Noordhoek Singapore.* She is 65.7 meters long and has a deck cargo capacity of 1,000 tons.

Lady Sandra is an example of a KMAR 404 type platform supply vessel built in 1998 by Kvaerner Kleven for the Australian Offshore services. Since the company entered into a joint venture with Farstad Shipping she has been under the Norwegian flag. Australian Offshore services is still part of the P&O empire and the style of naming their vessels has never changed even though the original parent company - International Offshore Services - is long gone.

Balblair is an example of a UT 705 pipe carrier designed and built by Ulstein shipyards and is one of a group of over 30 vessels. The design was revitalised in recent years and in later vessels the superstructure has been considerably enlarged. *Balblair* has a length of 80.8 meters and a deck cargo capacity of 2,180 tons. She was built in 1979 as *Tender Champion* for Wilhelmsen Offshore Services, becoming *Balblair* of BP Shipping Ltd. (Offshore Group) in 1985. Sold in 1993 she was renamed *Highland Champion.*

Highland Star is an example of a 'modernised' UT 705 pipe carrier now classed as a platform supply vessel. Although just over one meter longer than the original design, the deck cargo capacity has increased to 2,500 tons. She was built in 1990 by Brattvaag Skips as *Far Malin* for Farstad Shipping. Gulf Offshore Marine International Inc. bought her in 1991, renamed her *Highland Star* and registered her in the UK.

Royal Service was photographed at Hamilton on 20th June 1979. She and her sister *Regal Service* were built in 1976 by H. Suerken in Germany for Zapata. They were 76.9 meters long with a deck cargo capacity of 2,200 tons. Both were busily employed during the pipelay 'seasons' for many years in the North Sea but with the decline in pipelaying operations in recent years, *Royal Service* is now classed as a platform supply vessel. Her sister now operates as the *Namibian Gem*.

The pipe carrier *Princess Supplier* is seen at Montrose on 6th May 1988. One of a class of six by James Brown and Hamer in South Africa, four for Norwegian owners and two for the British Salvesens. She started life as the *Edda Sprint* in 1975 and, at the time of writing, has been renamed seven times, carrying four different names in 1990 alone. She is currently operating as the *Seabulk Martin 1*.

Taken at Aberdeen on 22nd July 1983, this view of the 1974-built pipe carrier *Thomasturm* clearly shows the sloping sides to the cargo deck bulwarks. Built for the Offshore Supply Association, she was renamed *OSA Aberdeen* in 1984 and was sold in 1989. Later in life this class of vessels was remodelled and re-classed as platform supply vessels due to the reduced demand for pipe carriers. She now operates as *Oxbridge*.

Skandi Marstein at Aberdeen on 31st July 1997. Only in recent years is there evidence that naval architects have given any sort of sweet lines to offshore support vessels. Here we see a 1996-built vessel from the yard of Brattvaag Skips which does show some efforts have been made to give her some 'shape'.

Conversions

A benefit of the flat, open after deck of a supply vessel is that it offers the perfect opportunity for conversion to other roles - whether short term or permanent. There have been occasions when truck-mounted cranes have been temporarily installed for specific lifting tasks. One of the heaviest and bulkiest cargoes recorded is that carried by a Smit-Lloyd vessel, a nuclear reactor of over 700 tons. There are also many instances of exceptional and irregular-shaped cargoes being carried. These are mainly prefabricated sections of steel jackets for offshore platforms being delivered to the main fabrication yards from those of subcontractors.

Perhaps the simplest conversion is that to a container carrier. The carriage of containers neatly stacked in tiers has also been recorded.

Various owners have opted to convert vessels in their fleets for specific uses. The most common are seismic survey, diving support, submersible support and oil well or platform maintenance. These conversions have been made by permanent additions of superstructure to the after deck to incorporate the necessary additional accommodation, laboratories, or workshops. In some cases heavy-lift capacity A frames have been installed at the stern which are capable of lifting small submersibles out of the water and setting them on cradles on the after deck.

In the case of diving support vessels, modifications have included the installation of a moon pool and decompression chamber as well as the equipment for lowering a diving bell to the seabed. The moon pool is a vertical rectangular shaft set in the hull that allows direct access to the water for men and equipment from the interior of the vessel rather than from the open deck.

For seismic survey work, part of the deck is taken up by the large winches and spools for the considerable lengths of cable that are streamed by the vessels in operational mode.

Possibly the simplest conversion of all is the removal of the bulwarks across the stern of a supply vessel in order to use it as a ferry. One company in the USA has bought second-hand supply vessels and carried out the conversions to vehicle ferries for a regular service from Woods Hole to Nantucket Island, one of the fleet being the *Katama.* Another example is the *Lady Rosalind,* which operates in the Bahamas and has been fitted with her own ramp and thus only needs a quay at which to berth. Similarly, the *Aries Tide* operates between Naples and the island of Capri.

After 10 years service as an anchor handling tug/supply vessel, the *Blue Flame 1* was sold and her new owners - Britannia Marine and Putford Enterprises - had her converted to a safety/stand-by vessel. Exceptionally, she is seen here at Hull on 15th August 1990 wearing the colours of British Gas - her operators at the time. She was built in 1976 as the *Star Pegasus* for Star Offshore Services

Originally Salvesen's South African-built *Highland Piper,* the 1977-vintage pipe carrier *Seaboard Coral* has been permanently converted to a safety/stand-by vessel. The conversion involved making an opening in her large bulwarks for access to the rescue zone. She was photographed at Hull on 3rd February 1993.

China Seal was built in 1977 as a supply vessel and was later converted for seismic survey work. This view at Aberdeen on 29th September 1996 clearly shows the modifications made.

Built in 1982 as the *Lady Pauline* for Australian Offshore Services, *Pacific Titan* was sold to Swire Pacific Offshore Services in 1986 and converted into a seismic survey vessel. The conversion was so drastic that she was actually widened by the use of sponsons.

Lady Gay at Singapore in 1990. Full circle - the vessel is being rebuilt as a fishing vessel. The supply vessel has gone back to its original roots after 16 years in the fleet of Australian Offshore Services.

Worldwide employment

Although reference has frequently been made to America and Europe; the actual search for offshore oil and gas has spread worldwide. It would not be an understatement to say that almost every country that has a coastline has been, at some point and in some way, involved in the massive industry that has developed. In the oil-rich states of the Arabian Gulf considerable deposits are in undersea fields. Further east, Indo-China, Indonesia, the Philippines, Australia and New Zealand are all rich in reserves, as are India, Pakistan, Bangladesh, Myanmar, Vietnam and Malaysia. Japan and a few countries in its neighbourhood seem to be the exception in not having reserves. China, on the other hand, has found considerable fields offshore. North Africa as well as almost the entire west coast of the continent has reserves. South America has deposits on both major coastlines. Canada and Mexico plus the Caribbean also have reserves. In fact, it may be easier to list the countries where oil and gas has not been located.

Therefore, many new fleets of offshore support vessels have developed over the years and at the same time the building of vessels has spread throughout the world. British, French, Danish, German, Polish, Finnish, Norwegian, Dutch, Belgian, Spanish, Italian, the former Yugoslavian, Romanian, Maltese, as well as shipyards in United States, Canada and Russia have built for the industry. Shipyards in Australia, China, Japan, Korea, Malaysia, Singapore, Thailand, Indonesia and India have built for either home use or for export. Offshore support vessels for service in Brazil have even been built at Manaus - 1,000 miles up the Amazon. Poland built almost an entire fleet of

vessels for Russia, which has now been broken down into smaller groups serving under the flags and colours of the newly-formed states of the former Soviet Union.

In many cases vessels displaced by more modern tonnage have been bought or transferred to new locations by their owners. Many dating from the 1960s can be found in the sunny, sheltered waters of the Middle and Far East. Others have been converted to safety-standby vessels to replace old sidewinder trawlers that positioned themselves in the vicinity of rigs and platforms. In recent years international legislation has precluded the older single-screw fishing vessels and their places have been taken up by the offshore support vessels, which have been modified for the purpose by having facilities added to act as rescue vessels. Some have even been equipped with additional azimuthing propulsion units to enable better station positioning.

Very few offshore support vessels have been scrapped in recent years. Some, built in the 1950s, are still in service; which is a tribute to their designers, builders and operators. In fact, the *Rip Tide*, which was built in 1955, was reported on the website of Marex Marine Services as being broken up in Morgan City as recently as 2001. The fate of the *Ebb Tide* is not clear except that she is known to have been transferred to Lake Maracaibo during her operational career with Tidewater Marine.

In fact, it may be fair to say that the wheel has gone full circle for many of the older supply vessels - especially in the United States - as they have returned to their roots and have been converted to fishing vessels.

Katama berthed at Woods Hole, USA. Built in 1982 as the supply vessel *Pro Navigator,* in the early 1990s this vessel was converted to a ferry for service to Nantucket Island. Loading is carried out over a shore-based ramp. She is not alone on this service as other similar conversions have been made. *Sankaty* is the latest member of this fleet.

Lady Rosalind entering Nassau. Built in 1979 as the *Misty Briley* for Briley Marine Services Inc., in 1984 she became *Gulf Fleet No. 301* for Zapata Gulf Marine Corp. In 1988 she was bought by Pirate Wells Investment Ltd. and fitted with a stern ramp for loading vehicles and construction equipment. Pirate Wells is a small island in the Bahamas, and Nassau is probably the source of most of her cargoes.

Terry O'Conallain supplied this photograph of the *Ariadne Alexandra* at Waterford, which he found, somewhat battered, on the floor of a warehouse in the city. Excuses for including it are that it follows up Ian Wilson's features on Irish ports and harbours, adds a footnote to the story of Capper, Alexander and Co. whose post-war fleet featured in *Record* 11, but most of all that it is an atmospheric shot of an obscure tramp.

Ariadne Alexandra was built in 1893 by William Gray and Co. Ltd. of West Hartlepool with machinery by their Central Marine Engine Works. Owner was the Ariadne Steamship Co. Ltd. of London, which is recorded as having slightly unusual funnel colours of a dark blue band between two pale blue bands on a basic black funnel. The photograph, however, appears to show two white bands.

It is intriguing to speculate on the geographical origins of those behind the ship. The first manager quoted is Michel Rodocanachi, although later George Sechiari and other Sechiaris are listed. Their surnames, and the overtones of Greek and Russian names combined to give *Ariadne Alexandra,* suggests that the owners might have moved to London from around the Black Sea from whence came much of Europe's grain. Here at Waterford, *Ariadne Alexandra* is unloading sacks, almost certainly of grain.

The ship was sold in 1910 to Capper, Alexander and Co., who soon registered her under the ownership of their Alexander Shipping Co. Ltd. although without changing her name. She survived the First World War and was broken up in 1932. The beaked stem is noteworthy: a sort of halfway house between the clipper bow and a straight stem.

PUTTING THE RECORD STRAIGHT

Letters, additions, amendments and photographs relating to articles in any issues of *Record* are welcomed. Letters may be lightly edited. E-mails are welcome, but senders are asked to include their postal address.

John Bowes: not the first author

I was interested in your article in *Record* 20 on *John Bowes* and her successors. As you suggest, other builders like Scott Russell (and Vernon and Mare) were building colliers at that time, but it was Palmer's links with the colliery owners that made it take off so quickly.

I would take slight issue with you on page 260 that 'No other author has been bold enough to describe *John Bowes* as the progenitor of the ocean-going tramp...' I wrote a paper for the Institution of Civil Engineers in 1969 identifying *John Bowes* as the first bulk carrier.

Dr IAN BUXTON,12 Grand Parade, Tynemouth, Tyne and Wear NE30 4JS.

As the senior association of engineers, the Institution of Civil Engineers has an excellent record of learned articles about shipping matters, and published the first discussion of the merits of the steam collier in a paper by Allen in 1854. Ed.

Chiefly concerning colliers

John Bowes (*Record* 20). I think it is clear that *Haggerstone* (415/1852) had the first double bottom ballast tanks: see my 'Steam Collier Fleets', page 13. McIntyre tanks can be retrofitted fairly easily as the structure runs longitudinally over the existing frames, unlike a cellular double bottom which requires each floor to be deeper.

John Bowes did not get a compound engine until 1883, the 1864 machinery was an in-line twin-cylinder simple engine. There were bearing and other problems with the 'V' type engines originally fitted to colliers as they ran twice as fast as the engines of paddle steamers, and the makers were on a steep learning curve. Efficient screw speeds were around 60 rpm, paddle speeds half this. Although screw engines had been around for some time, they had been heavily sail assisted, and even when not actually disconnected much of the load comes off the engine bearings when the sails are pulling.

In the photograph of *John Bowes* on page 256, I am sure the structure is a boom rigged to hold the staging, which has no stays attached. The number of plate strakes is noteworthy: the iron plates used on early ships were not very wide.

Collier (page 254) is shown after she was rebuilt and had a forecastle added sometime after the turn of the century. Bristol photo P4300M shows her approaching the entrance locks before she was rebuilt: I drew the sketch of her on page 45 of 'Steam Coasters' from this photograph. *Collier* was chartered to H.P. Maples from about 1854 to 1857 for his services in connection with the Newhaven services of the London, Brighton and South Coast Railway. According to B.M.E. O'Mahoney in 'Newhaven-Dieppe 1825-1980' also chartered were the screw colliers *William Cory*, *Samuel Laing* and *James Dixon*. Maples must have been using them for cargo or possibly other trades, although deck passengers were permitted then, just like cattle! Of course, they could have been delivering bunker coal.

'150 years of colliers' (*Record* 21). I think *J.R. Hinde* would have had a rig like *Weardale* and *William Cory* (the photograph of the latter was almost certainly taken around 1857 as she is dressed overall). In the late-in-life picture of *J.R. Hinde* the topmasts have been cut right down but the tell-tale crosstrees remain and must have supported lofty topmasts. The derricks seem to have been removed, too. It is unusual to have just a foresail and this would only be of use when running or reaching - perhaps it was the only sail left at the end of her life. What would be expected is the balanced rig of *Tanfield*. All except the mizzen boom have been discarded, probably because of grab discharge. The work boat may well have been placed in davits on the starboard rail. However, vessels of the period did carry boats in this manner and, as discharge was largely manual, the boats were probably not in the way. They would only be a problem if the ship was forced to dock with the boat to the quay or staith.

Eastwood looks as if she still has her original-length fidded topmasts, but the picture is rather too small to be sure. 1870 would be early for pole masts, which brings me to *Usworth* which clearly has pole masts. But take a close look at the mizzen, does it have a small topmast? The other interesting feature is what I presume to be a deck crane in front of the bridge. *Usworth* also has two hatches rather than one long hatch and bulwark doors are clearly visible in contrast to *John Bowes*.

Medway has similarly been cut down: she has the shortest topmasts I have ever seen. I think the mizzen pole mast may be original.

Dr. CHARLES WAINE, Mount Pleasant, Beamish Lane, Albrighton, Wolverhampton WV7 3JJ

It is gratifying to have it confirmed that John Bowes *was not initially fitted with McIntyre tanks. Captain A.W. Kinghorn has written to point out that a respected author, Roger Finch in 'Coals from Newcastle', implies - wrongly it is now believed - that she had a double bottom from new. The statement on page 258 of the* Record *article on* John Bowes *that she was fitted with a compound engine in 1862 was an error; the history of the ship on page 260 gives the correct story. Ed.*

I have looked at the Lloyd's Survey Reports (LSR) and you might like to add the following to the information given in *Record* 21:

Lady Alice Lambton (LSR reference IRN458) surveyed on the slip at Shields on 18th March 1853. As first surveys are carried out before the vessel enters service this puts a question mark against the date of the maiden voyage, unless for some obscure reason the vessel entered service uninsured, carried out one round voyage and was then re-slipped for the survey to be undertaken. The engines are shown to be 88 HP.

Rouen (LSR IRN1767) surveyed 15th September 1857 and engines shown to be 80 HP.

J.R. Hinde (LSR IRN3580) surveyed 14th May 1864 and engines shown to be 90 HP.

Tanfield (LSR IRN3956) surveyed 17th January 1865 (launched 14th December 1864) and engines are shown to be 95 HP.

On Page 31, top photo, the vessel is the *Boleslaw Bierut,* not *Boleslaw Beirut* as shown in the heading and caption. Also on page 31 the bottom photo is given as the *Vassil Levsky* and this is how the vessel's name is spelt in all of the registers, but the name on the bow of the ship appears to be *Vasil Levsky*.

David Hodge has asked me to point out a small error in *Record* 20. On page 238 the name of the salvage vessel involved with the *Ben-My-Chree* was not *Vallette*. It should be *La Valette*. She had a long career, being built by Mitchell and Co. Ltd. at Newcastle in 1879 as the *Nora*, subsequently being renamed *Hiawatha*, then *Clara*, then *Hiawatha*, then yacht *Polygon* before becoming the *La Valette* in about 1916-1917. In 1932 she was sold to a Turkish company and was renamed *Lavalet*, becoming *Akbas* in 1935. She is in the 1947-48 'Lloyd's Register' but not in the 1948-49 edition. Presumably scrapped.

David Hodge has also pointed out that the number quoted for the photograph of Harrison's *Craftsman* on page 195 of *Record* 16 was wrong: the correct negative number is N47921.

BOB TODD, National Maritime Museum, Greenwich, London SE10 9NF

Which is correct, the name painted on the ship or the name given in 'Lloyd's Register'? The name of a ship given in 'Lloyd's Register' is usually taken from official sources, such as the country's official register. This is more likely to reflect the owner's intention as to how the name is spelt than the work of the seaman or shipbuilder who painted it on the bow. With Bulgaria, which uses the cyrillic script, the name rendered in Roman characters is a transliteration, giving further possibility for error. John B. Hill has pointed out that the Vassil Levsky, *as* Granpond, *was not converted from a merchant aircraft carrier to a cargo ship when sold to Goulandris in 1946, but was laid up at Barrow until 1951. After renaming* Condor *she was towed to Hamburg for conversion in January 1951, the work being completed in June.* Lady Alice Lambton *was registered on 5th April 1853, so could not have made her maiden voyage in February 1853 as stated in the article. Ed.*

I have read your collier article in *Record* 21 with interest, and in particular *J.R. Hinde* (page 38) wherein you compare her after bulwarks with those on *Tanfield*. I would offer the suggestion that *J.R. Hinde* may have had her after bulwarks 'solidified' during her conversion for towing jury lighters on the Goole run. If you look at the after end you can clearly see the tow bow and towing hook that were added. She was the first company vessel so converted for that purpose. It is, however, only a suggestion as there is no earlier photographic proof of which I am aware.
BILL HARVEY, 36 Renals Street, Mill Hill, Derby DE3 6SH

It was interesting to see *Sylvia Beale* pictured in your '150 Years of Colliers' feature. Although she, and her two sisters *Eleanor Brooke* and *Elizabeth Lysaght* were typical 'Shoreham-max' vessels of their day, it has always been my understanding that the trio were built with another trade in mind, that of transporting steel ingots etc, between the steelworks of Scunthorpe (via the Trent, or maybe Immingham), and Port Talbot. Depending on which direction the steel was carried, the round trip would be completed with a coal cargo from either Goole or Port Talbot, to Shoreham. I do not know who the Beales or Brookes were, but the Lysaghts were, I believe, a leading steelmaking family, hence the choice of name for that vessel.
JOHN LINGWOOD, 52 Nursery Road, Sunderland SR3 1NT
Correspondent and contributor John B. Hill also queried the trades for which these three colliers were intended, pointing out that Stephenson Clark rarely gave their ships peoples' names. He never saw the small derricks on these ships used for taking in stores, save for taking on board new mooring ropes, but they were useful for handling the small wooden dinghies in which the crew would go ashore when the ship happened to be anchored in mid-stream or moored at buoys. Mr G. Weaver has pointed out that the length of Sylvia Beale was 211 feet, not as shown in her caption. Ed.

The shot of the old *Eastwood* in ice on the Thames (*Record* 21, page 39) is superbly interesting, although that sailing vessel is a brigantine, not a brig (fore and aft rigged mainmast). The goosewinged topsail schooner further upriver has caught a slant of wind, probably with the tide helping her along. Inbound sailing vessels would often anchor on an adverse tide, then pick up when the flood made. Whilst being my usual pedantic self, I will mention that the horizontal spar from which a squaresail is set is the *yard*. Only the yard's outer ends, port and starboard, are the *yardarms*.

The Irish port pictures are also superb, the beached brigantine on page 50 being particularly interesting as she has a bentick boom on the foremast. I think this was to keep the foot of the fore lower squaresail stretched taut for river work, as the sails would be backed and filled when rounding the bends - they were a notable feature on the Geordie colliers where river work would be similar to that on the Quoile.

On page 57 that elegant shot of the 1977 *Manchester Venture* shows clearly how her lines were used as a basis for Blue Star's boxboats *Australia Star* and *New Zealand Star* built at Haverton Hill soon afterwards. That much of the preliminary paper work - for instance, calculations and drawings - had already been done, made the tender price offered entirely acceptable when the order was placed. The Blue Stars had slightly different dimensions and were refrigerated vessels, but the basic similarities are there to see in your photograph. We were told they were built to a Manchester Liners' design.
CAPTAIN A.W. KINGHORN, 15 Kendal Avenue, Cullercoats, North Shields, Tyne & Wear NE30 3AQ

Colour blind
With respect to Alan Phipps letter 'Kulukundis kolours' in *Record* 21, I am surprised that it did not warrant a note from the editor and very surprised that the mistake to which it refers had gone unnoticed because in 'Marine News' for June 1978, volume 32, No. 6 on page 272 an article entitled 'Aegean Mariners' by R.S. Fenton features the funnel colours. It also refers to 'Ships Loved and Painted' by Manuel E.Kulukundis edited by J.A. Hadjipateras in which he states that the 'K' was red whist the paintings of the *Atlantis* and *Mount Atlas* clearly shows a blue letter. A case of Irish-Greeks?
A. D. FROST, 32 Oakfield Close, Sunderland, Tyne and Wear SR33RT

Sunderland collier in focus
I was interested in the photograph on page 184 of *Record* 19 showing colliers at Sunderland in June 1953. The Donking collier behind *Westburn* would appear to be the *Dona Flora* (1,179/1924; 201 feet). She was sold in 1956 to the Holderness Steamship Co. Ltd., Hull as *Holdernett* and scrapped at Troon in 1957. Her sister *Dona Isabel* was sunk by an E-boat on 2nd November 1943.
G. WEAVER, 56 Coulsdon Rise, Coulsdon, Surrey CR5 2SB

Dona Flora had a profile that was almost unique amongst coastal tramp steamers. Whereas the enormous majority of steamers of her size had a raised forecastle and quarterdeck, giving a short well forward, she was flush-decked aft of the forecastle. Although used mainly for tramping by T.H. Donking and Sons Ltd. of Middlesbrough, she was ordered from the Furness Shipbuilding Co. Ltd., Haverton Hill-on-Tees for a cargo liner service to Portugal. *[Roy Fenton collection]*

All about Granges

Correspondents have made a number of additions and corrections to the articles on Houlder's post-war Granges.

Page 130 of Record 19: the second paragraph reads, 'From 1899 until the demise of Houlder Line Ltd. in 1974 all the Granges were registered under the ownership of Houlder Line Ltd....' Bill Laxon points out that the Oswestry Grange of 1902 was registered to the Oswestry Grange Steam Ship Co. Ltd. and the Everton Grange of 1903 to the Empire Transport Co. Ltd. and both so remained until sold in 1911/12 to the New Zealand Shipping Co. Ltd. There may well have been others.

Page 139: the Antartico was substantially rebuilt with a new superstructure following her conversion to diesel power. A photo in her rebuilt form appears in 'Sea Breezes', 1951, Volume 12, page 457.

Page 195 of Record 20: the net tonnage of Rippingham Grange was 6,239n.

Dunster Grange *was renamed Vaasa by the Finnish company which bought her in 1951, not Vasa.*

Page 198: Elstree Grange as Samettrick was managed by the Peninsular and Oriental Steam Navigation Company. P&O never has been Ltd.; it is incorporated by Royal Charter.

The later owner of Barton Grange was Pan Norse without a u.

Page 200: Thorpe Grange was renamed St Merriel for five years from 1966 to 1971 as well as the 14 months from 1972 to 1973.

Page 201: Denby Grange had two turbines, as had the Royston Grange and Hardwicke Grange.

Page 202: author John B. Hill has pointed out that the Oswestry Grange was not waiting to load, and that the condition of the hull paint was due to her having been laid up for eight months on account of the miners' strike in 1984. During this period there was only a skeleton crew on board, so maintenance was minimal.

The builders' yard number of Hardwick Grange was 744.

Page 204: *since the articles were published the Upwey Grange as Orgullo has been reported sold to Indian shipbreakers for $780,000.*

Page 205: the tonnage of Hornby Grange was 39,629g.

Page 206: the name of the grange close to Little Weighton is actually Riplingham, not Rippingham.

The owners of Dunster Grange (usually called castle) were the Luttrell family.

Not about Granges

Congratulations on the publication of the twentieth issue of Ships in Focus *Record,* and here's looking forward to at least another twenty issues. I've enjoyed reading all the articles and viewing the photos of the many varied vessels. Niceties over now a bit of criticism!

Having been employed as a shore-gang rigger, in the

Dennis Johnzon, ever alert for matters pertaining to Houlders, has kindly supplied this photograph of the *Bore IX,* which was featured as *Queensbury* on page 62 of *Record* 21. Comparison with the photo as *Queensbury* shows she has been substantially rebuilt. *[Real Photographs Co. Ltd.]*

Royal Group of Docks during the 1960s and 1970s working on the Houlder boats, I very much enjoyed John B. Hill's article. But, why was poor old *Duquesa* left out? OK, she was not a Grange boat but I feel her inclusion would have completed the fleet of 'fridge boats on the London to River Plate run of the period mentioned. A picture of *Duquesa* would have shown her to be the 'in between' stage of the gradual design from the *Hornby Grange* to the *Royston Grange* class of vessel. She also had the largest gross tonnage of her contemporaries.

Although I was working for Blue Star at the time of the *Royston Grange* tragedy, the feeling throughout the shore gangs in the Royal Docks was that we had lost one of 'our' ships and crew. JW GRAINGER, 'Kyrenia', Second Avenue, Brentwood, Essex CM15 OHH

The simple answer to the question why John Hill left Duquesa out of his article is that she did not have a Grange name. In fact, she like some of the Granges came from a long line of Houlder meat ships, and it is hoped to cover these in a future issue of Record. Ed.

Sure, what would we be doin' if she sank?

Just received *Record* 21 - I feel that the pages devoted to Ellermans are just about right.

I found the photo of the *Belturbet,* on page 48 delightful - talk about Health and Safety! I counted at least 75 people on the upper deck, with more below, the life saving apparatus appears to be a lifeboat slung over the transom with a capacity of about 10 to 15. Whether she had any buoyant apparatus in addition I do not know, but had she met with an accident the passengers would have been in trouble. As for the gangway, a modern safety inspector would have a fit! Just goes to show what the world was like before our litigious times.

What a fine looking ship the *Zaandijk* was (page 60). Any mileage in a future feature on cargo ships with clipper bows, bowsprits and figureheads? [*Any offers?* Ed.]

A couple of minor comments - the *Battersea* (page 46) is passing under Westminster Bridge, not Waterloo Bridge. *Lawhill* (page 29) was broken up in Lourenco Marques in 1957, when she had deteriorated into a rotting hulk. Her remains were loaded as scrap into the holds of the South African Railway's *Dahlia,* herself to be broken up on arrival at the scrappers at Kobe.

TONY SMYTHE, 35 Avondale Road, Rayleigh, Essex SS6 8NJ

Notes on 19 ...

Page 144: I assume that the comments on this page refer only to the post-war Bank ships. The pre-war Harland-B&W-engined ships did not have opposed piston machinery and the four ships built by Workman Clark in 1930 (*Irisbank, Lossiebank, Taybank* and *Tweedbank*) all had Workman Clark-Sulzer diesels, which were single acting, not opposed piston.

Page 146: *Westbank.* The text refers to her having a four-cylinder Doxford diesel whereas the photo caption refers to a five-cylinder engine. The latter is correct.

P.157: *Blythe Star.* Ruwolt's works were in Melbourne. She did not have a 12-cylinder engine, but was twin screw with two six-cylinder engines.

Page 158: *Claire Crouch.* The Crossley engine was not installed until 1950. Previous to that she had a two-cylinder engine by N.V. Steywal-Motorenfabrik of Overschie. She was first registered in Australia at Port Adelaide in May 1923 for Yorke Shipping Pty. Ltd.

Page 167: The two *Gafsa* photos. My first reaction was that perhaps the sinking photo was of the second *Gafsa* ex-*Dominion* of 1901 which Bowrings renamed after the loss of the first *Gafsa.* She herself was lost in 1917. But it cannot be her because the *Gafsa* ex-*Dominion* had three masts, a three-island hull and engines aft. *U 35* seems to have been a singularly successful submarine with something over 70 ships sunk, mostly in the Mediterranean. I cannot reconcile any of her other victims with the ship in the photo (assuming it is another victim of *U 35*), but there are a number of these of which I do not have photos to make a comparison. It will be interesting to see if anyone comes up with the answer.

Page 174: *Clansman.* There is no 'e' on the end of Clark in the name of her builders. I know that 'Lloyd's Register' consistently gives her engine builders as J. Rowan and Co. but I have never come across such a firm anywhere else. Should it not be D. (for David) Rowan, who remained a well-known Glasgow engine builder into the 1960s, latterly as a Fairfield/Lithgow subsidiary?

Page 178: A stray letter d seems to have crept into the name of the *Munisa.*

...and tweaks to 20

Page 234: *Empress Queen.* She was built in 1897, not 1907, as correctly recorded on Page 234.

Congratulations on a well researched and most interesting article on the *John Bowes.* I agree with your argument that she is the forerunner of the modern bulker.

Page 260: The *Connaught* of 1860 was not 'Royal Mail' as that term is generally understood - i.e. RMSP Co. She belonged to the Atlantic Royal Mail Steam Navigation Company, generally known as the Galway Line.

BILL LAXON, Waimarama, Upper Whangateau Road, PO Box 171, Matakana 1240, New Zealand.

Detentions for Kinghorn

On pages 34/35 of *Record* 21, Captain Kinghorn writes about the vessels detained because of the political problems in the Balkans. He has missed two ships that were detained and they were in British waters! The Yugoslavia bulk carriers *Pomorac* and *Radnik* were detained in the River Fal. The *Pomorac* arrived on 24th November 1992 and sailed as the *Grant Carrier* on 12th March 1996. The *Radnik* arrived on the 29th November 1992, she sailed as the *Grant Trader* on 18th March 1996.

Secondly, on page 57 you bring your readers up to date with the Manchester Liners container ships. In *Marine News* for August 2002 page 498 it is reported that the *Manchester Vanguard* and *Manchester Venture* have just gone to the breakers in India. These two ships where also laid up in the Fal. The *Manchester Vanguard* laid up on the 25th July 1980 and sailed on 26th September the same year. Her sistership the *Manchester Venture* laid up on the 4th August 1980 and sailed on the 14th September. The *Manchester Vanguard* returned to lay up as the *Oriental Vanguard* on the 24th January 1981 and she sailed from the River Fal on 19th April 1981. The *Manchester Reward* also laid up in the Fal from 13th July 1981 to 26th August 1918.

TONY ATKINSON, 'Tregarth', 20 Lower Redannick, Truro, Cornwall TR1 2JW

T is for Tuillier

Recently I've received the once again outstanding Ships In Focus *Record* 21. I've seen a small mistake in the *Hudson Firth* history. In 1967 she was purchased by the Compania de Navegacion 'Rivabell' S.A. (Lugano), Panama. Behind this company was Sebastiano Tuillier, which had almost the same funnel mark as the Tsavrilis Group. Tuillier was Italian and emigrated to Lugano in Switzerland, that is also the reason why the ship bore the name *Lugano.* Sebastiano Tuillier also owned in the late 1940s and early 1950s *San Salvatore* (5,591/1919) and *Generoso* (1,552/1913) under the Swiss flag.

MARKUS BERGER, Amselweg 13, CH-8302 Kloten, Switzerland
Markus alerted us to a website which he helped construct, www.swiss-ships.ch. With detailed histories and excellent photographs of Swiss ships, it is well worth visiting. Ed.

Tazzy traders revisited

On page 156 of the Ships in Focus *Record* 19 there was a feature on Tasmanian traders out of Hobart. The photo on page 156 of the Hobart wharves named the ships *Port Townsville, Karoon* and *Adelong.*

The large vessel on the north side of Kings Wharf was one of the four ships transferred to the Canadian-Union Line Ltd. in 1946. They were built in 1944 for the Canadian Government in Vancouver and were managed by Park Steamship Co. Ltd. The ships were *Waikawa* (3), *Waitomo* (2), *Wairuna* (3), and *Waihemo* (3), all of the 10,000 deadweight Park design. The four ships were used on a monthly service between West Coast Pacific Ports - Pacific Islands - New Zealand - Australia. They were transferred to Wellington registry in 1950 and were sold for further trading between 1959 and 1966.

Keep up the good work with *Record.*
BOB SILBERBERG, 22 Ernest Street, Beauty Point 7270, Tasmania, Australia
The four former Parks are illustrated in Ian Farquhar's recently published 'Union Fleet'. Ed.

Ballast fraud

Congratulations on another splendid issue of *Record* - No. 21, in which I particularly enjoyed the article on the *Inveravon* by John Naylon. In mentioning the notorious nature of the Callao shingle ballast, and the fact that a number of vessels had mysteriously disappeared after loading ballast at Callao, there was another contributory factor that was perhaps more relevant and should also be noted. The following is extracted from Captain James S. Learmont's book 'A Master in Sail'.

'When sailing the four-masted barque *Bengairn* into Callao, Captain James Learmont was well aware of the notice issued by the British Consulate to shipmasters concerning the ballast, and took the necessary precautions of erecting double shifting boards and extra securing measures, and when ordering the ballast he also made the local (English) Harbour Master aware of his intention to weigh samples of the ballast during loading. This caused quite a stir locally and the word got round so that about a dozen British shipmasters turned up to witness the event. It was during the subsequent loading that it became clear to Captain Learmont that he was being under-delivered by a fair amount - in fact according to his calculations he was approximately 14% down on the 1,000 tons his vessel required and had ordered, in something that was vital to the ship's safety.

Before Captain Learmont would sign for the delivery, he insisted on receiving the full amount, and eventually loaded the extra ballast necessary to complete the 1,000 tons required. He continues 'following my fight no other ship was posted missing after leaving Callao - if a fight had been put up sooner it would be safe to say that the *Cape York, Dominion, Dunreggan* and *Dalgonar,* besides many other others would not have been lost'.

It is obvious that if given short weight, the ship was liable to heel to a dangerous degree and in so doing would cause the ballast to run.

Since reading *Record* I am able to look at ship photographs with a far more inquisitive and questioning eye, and John Naylon's articles are excellent, the story of these vessels - together with the men that sailed in them - must not be forgotten.

TONY WESTMORE, 29 Queens Road, Cowes, Isle of Wight P031 8BW

Bank engines

I spent all my working life with Andrew Weir Co. Ltd.'s Bank Line and my interest in the company continued in my retirement. I commenced my apprenticeship on deck on joining the motor vessel *Westbank* at Doxford's Pallion yard in November 1948. Although not a member of the engine department my three years on this ship ensured that I became familiar with all her aspects. In the very good article on Bank Line engines in *Record* 19 there is an error relating to the description of the oil engines fitted in the motor vessels *Eastbank*, *Westbank* and *Southbank* as being four-cylinder. These ships, with a service speed of 14 knots, were fitted with five-cylinder engines as stated in the caption beneath the photograph of the *Westbank*.

The first motorships constructed by Doxford for Andrew Weir were a series of three built in 1937. These were the *Eskbank*, *Teesbank* and *Ettrickbank* and it was this series that was fitted with four-cylinder engines. The only three-cylinder Doxford-engined ships built for the company were *Willowbank* in 1939 (torpedoed and lost in 1940), *Roybank* and *Weybank* in 1944, and the *Meadowbank* and *Moraybank* in 1945. In 1943 the Ministry of War Transport built a three-legged Doxford-engined ship at Pallion, the *Empire City*, managers Andrew Weir and Co. Ltd., and had she not been torpedoed in 1944 one would have imagined that she would have joined the post-war fleet of the Bank Line.

Generally I found *Record* 19 to be of considerable interest but feel that, in the pages dedicated to Bank engines, a little more could have been written about William Doxford and the Pallion Yard with particular reference to the new undercover facility constructed in the mid-1970s, the very existence and success of which was entirely dependent upon the Andrew Weir order for six general-purpose cargo liners of over 16,000 tons deadweight. These orders were followed by a further two at over 18,000 tons deadweight each and then the six 'Fish-class' ships each of over 18,000 tons deadweight, three coming from the undercover yard and three being traditionally slipway constructed.

The briefest reference was made to a single container ship. This was the 1980-built refrigerated container motor ship *Willowbank* from Smith's Dock, Middlesbrough, engined by Kincaid, Burmeister & Wain. She was the last ship to be built for the company before the Bank Line Ltd. changed its name to Andrew Weir Shipping Ltd. when MacAndrews and United Baltic Corporation became fully integrated into the group and before the Ellerman interests were absorbed.

ALAN BURROUGHS, 25 Ewan Way, Leigh-on-Sea, Essex SS9 3RA

Starboard out, starboard home?

Many congratulations to *Record* on reaching its 21st issue, can it really be six years since No.1 came through the letterbox? You said in the first preface that you had identified a niche for high quality articles supported by equally high quality photographs, and you have succeeded admirably in both ... thanks must go to every contributor as well as the editorial team. But, and there is always a but (!), are we also to congratulate the Skyfotos photographer for the splendid starboard-side view of *City of Manchester* which graces the cover and page 2 of *Record* 21, more especially as he has seemingly caught her port side in identical pose, even with the same fishing boat abreast No.2 hatch, as reproduced across the front and back cover? And her name is running the right way on bow and bridge wing! Surely *Record* could not engage in any sort of photographic skullduggery ... can we trust you for the next 21 issues?
GEORGE ROBINSON, Southwood Cottage, 79 Southwood Road, Cottingham, East Yorkshire HU16 5AJ
In the right hands, Adobe Photoshop can do wonders. Ed.

Gas pioneer

The *Clerk-Maxwell* (*Record* 20, page 212) was of a pioneer design and the first gas carrier built for Ocean Gas Transport Co. Ltd. She had a number of teething troubles and her relatively early demise - she was sold to Spanish breakers at the age of 20 years - was occasioned by a structural deficiency which would have been expensive to rectify.
JOHN B. HILL, The Hollies, Wall, Hexham, Northumberland NE46 4EQ

Bank Line motorships have been given a very good airing in recent editions of *Record*, and to wind this up here are some of the earlier Doxford diesel-engined ships.

Below: Andrew Weir's first Doxford motorship was *Eskbank* (5,137/1937), actually owned by his Inver Transport and Trading Co. Ltd. rather than Bank Line. She was sold to Hong Kong owners in 1961 to become *Hsin Ann*, and survived until 1967 when she was broken up at Singapore.

Opposite upper: *Roybank* (7,368/1944) was a wartime completion with a Doxford three-cylinder engine. In 1962 she too was sold to a Hong Kong owner, C.S. Koo, who renamed her *Silver Lake* under the Liberian flag. She was broken up in Taiwan in 1968.

Opposite lower: delivered by the same yard, with a similar Doxford engine only eight months after *Roybank*, the *Moraybank* (7,307/1945) had a distinctly different profile, more reminiscent of the 'B' type standard steam tramps built for the Ministry of War Shipping. She was sold in 1962, once again to Hong Kong owners but now in the shape of Mullion and Co. Ltd., who renamed her first *Ardrowan* and later *Tetrarch*. Hong Kong breakers began demolishing her late in 1969. [All: A. Duncan]

SOURCES AND ACKNOWLEDGEMENTS
Photographs are from the collection of John Clarkson unless otherwise credited. We thank all who gave permission for their photographs to be used, and for help in finding photographs we are particularly grateful to Tony Smith, Jim McFaul and David Whiteside of the World Ship Photo Library; to Ian Farquhar, Bill Laxon, Peter Newall, Ivor Rooke, William Schell, George Scott; to David Hodge and Bob Todd of the National Maritime Museum; Dr. David Jenkins of the National Museums and Galleries of Wales; and other museums and institutions listed.

Research sources have included the *Registers* of William Schell and Tony Starke, *Lloyd's Register, Lloyd's Confidential Index, Lloyd's War Losses, Mercantile Navy Lists,* and *Marine News.* Use of the facilities of the World Ship Society's Central Record, the Guildhall Library, the Public Record Office and Lloyd's Register of Shipping are gratefully acknowledged. Particular thanks also to William Schell and John Bartlett for various information, to Heather Fenton for editorial and indexing work, and to Marion Clarkson for accountancy services.

CULTURE SHOCK ON THE COAST
Particular thanks to Ken Garrett. An article by Gil Mayes on Empire Fs in 'Coastal Shipping' for February 2002 was also consulted.

ORSVs
All the pictures in these articles are from the author's collection which has been augmented from gifts, purchases or copies made in agreement with the original photographers. Special thanks go to Jim Prentice, Mike Smith, Andrew Wiltshire, Albert Novelli, Jim Charnock, Fred Kissack, Matt McKay, Jim McFaul and John Clarkson.

LOOSE ENDS
Details of *Gondolier* and *Glengarry* from: CLD Duckworth and GE Langmuir *West Highland Steamers,* Richard Tilling, London, 1950

BLAIRSPEY
Many thanks to David Burrell for sharing his information on the Nisbets and their fleet and to Mrs Jean McCormick for details of her husband's service on *Blairspey.* Other books consulted were:

Blair, Clay. *Hitler's U-boat War: the Hunters 1939-1942.* Random House, New York, 1996.
Mitchell WH and Sawyer LA. *The Empire Ships.* Second edition. Lloyds of London, London, 1990.
Rohwer J. *Axis Submarine Successes 1939-1945.* Patrick Stephens, Cambridge, 1983
Thomas, PN *British Ocean Tramps Volume 2. Owners and their ships.* Waine Research Publications, Albrighton, 1992

FROM Z TO Z: A SELECTION OF TURNER, BRIGHTMAN SHIPS
Partcular thanks to Kevin O'Donoghue, Ivor Rooke and David Hodge of the National Maritime Museum, without whom this feature would not have been possible

Middlemiss, NL *Travels of the Tramps, volume 2.* Shield Publications, Newcastle, 1991
Thomas, PN *British Ocean Tramps Volume 2. Owners and their ships.* Waine Research Publications, Albrighton, 1992

A NEW LEASE OF LIFE FOR *LYRIA*
Peter Myers

The conversion of American-built, war standard T2 tankers to dry cargo bulk carriers was fairly commonplace in the late 1950s and early 1960s. These conversions, which often involved lengthening and the installation of cargo-handling gear, gave a new lease of life to some of the T2s and a few could still be found trading in the mid-1970s. One of the last to be seen in British waters was the *Santa Elia*, which had been built as the *White River* in 1944. She had been 'jumboised' for her new role as a dry cargo bulk carrier in 1959, but her career was destined to end in ignominy when she was placed under arrest at Liverpool in 1975. The Panamanian-registered *Santa Elia* was sold by court order to Spanish shipbreakers and arrived at Bilbao in March 1976 for demolition.

A year earlier another former tanker converted to a dry cargo bulk carrier also arrived at a Spanish port to be broken up. She was the *Yebala*, which had been built as the Anglo-Saxon Petroleum Company's *Lyria* in 1946 and was a near-contemporary of the T2s. She was one of the rare examples of a British-built tanker to undergo such a conversion and in her new role outlasted her sister-ship *Linga* by 12 years. The *Lyria* and *Linga* were among the first of Anglo-Saxon's post-war L class, which were built between 1946 and 1948 and were of 6,400 gross tons. The *Lyria* was launched at Harland and Wolff's yard at Belfast on 6th March 1946 and was delivered to her owners on 20th June that year. Delivery of the *Linga* followed on 19th September. Their dimensions were 446 feet by 55 feet and they carried a deadweight of 9,297 tons at 12 knots on a draught of 25 feet 8 inches. They were propelled by oil engines designed and made at the builder's workshops in Belfast.

The L class helped make good Shell's war losses, but the Shell fleet was expanding and within a few years the first supertankers were joining the fleet. The V class included the *Verena* (18,654/1950), which came from Harland and Wolff at Belfast and could carry 75 per cent more than the largest Shell tanker in service at the time. The new supertankers made the *Lyria* and her sisters seem quite small fry, and it is not surprising that Shell Tankers Ltd. sold the *Lyria* in 1955 to Union Atlantico SA, whose managing owner was M. Yllera, of Santander, Spain. The *Lyria's* comparatively brief spell in the oil trades had seen the world's tanker fleet grow from 1,768 ships of 21 million tons in 1945 to 2,693 of 39 million tons in 1955.

Harland and Wolff Ltd. contributed exactly half of the 12-strong L class to Anglo-Saxon's fleet, including *Lyria* (above) and *Linga* (right). Most of these motor tankers had very short lives, for instance after only 11 years' service *Lepton* (6,446/1947) was laid up in October 1958, and was broken up two years later. Sale of *Lyria* as early as 1955 suggests their owners had realised the class was destined for a short life. *Linga* (6,452/1946) was one of the longer-lived, being demolished in Belgium in 1963, although still only 17 years old. Yet as the conversion of *Lyria* to a bulker showed, the hulls and engines of these tankers were good for many more years. *[Both: Fotoflite incorporating Skyfotos]*

Top: the high hatch-coamings help identify *Yebala* as a dry cargo bulk carrier. Conversion from a tanker also involved removal of the topmasts. [J. and M. Clarkson]

Middle and bottom: the Aberdeen Harbour Board's tugs *Sea Griffon* and *Sea Trojan* bring the *Yebala* up the navigation channel after her arrival from Dakar on 12th June 1972, and manoeuvre her alongside the deepwater Pacific Wharf. The Yllera family's distinctive funnel colours – black with a white band carrying a red zig-zag stripe – can be clearly seen in the latter view. The Yllera's are reported to have had an equally striking houseflag, comprising a white ground with, at the top, half of a red ball with seven 'rays' radiating from it downwards and to the side, like a sun. This was recorded in Colin Stewart *Flags, Funnels and Hull Colours* (Adlard Coles, Southampton, 1962), but has never been seen in the wild, i.e. flown from a ship. [Both Peter Myers]

The *Lyria* was renamed *Yebala*, which was in Spanish Morocco, and she was registered at Rio Martin. Senor Yllera had a new role for his new acquisition and in 1956 the *Yebala* was converted to a dry cargo bulk carrier, having a new gross tonnage of 4,698 tons. In 1957, her managing owner became Angel Yllera of Santander, and Panama became her port of registry. In 1961 there was another change when her owning company became the Atlantic Union Corporation, although still owned by the Yllera family, and in 1964 her port of registry was changed to Monrovia, Liberia.

I first encountered the *Yebala* in June 1972 when she was lying in Aberdeen Bay waiting for the pilot and the help of Aberdeen Harbour Board's two tugs to bring her into port. She had arrived from Dakar/Senegal, with a cargo of phosphate imported by Scottish Agricultural Industries Ltd. for the manufacture of compound fertiliser at its Aberdeen works. The *Yebala's* profile still resembled that of a traditional, three-island tanker, but her new role was indicated by her prominent hatch coamings.

The tugs *Sea Griffon* and *Sea Trojan* brought the *Yebala* bow first up the navigation channel before swinging her round so that she was berthed stern first at the deepwater Pacific Wharf. Discharge of her cargo soon got under way and on 15th June, 3,000 tons of phosphate were discharged from her in one day, which was a record for the port. She returned to Aberdeen in October 1972 and February 1973, and later in 1973 she was due at Avonmouth in September from Dakar, most likely with phosphate. It was from Avonmouth that she sailed on 15th February 1975 on her last voyage, destined for Aviles, Spain, where breakers Desguaces Aviles began work on her at San Juan de Nieva, Aviles, on 8th March 1975.

The *Yebala* had enjoyed a 20-year career in the bulk trades and the Yllera family seemed to have maintained her in good condition during that period. She could still be identified as a former Shell tanker and her funnel markings of a red zig-zag on a broad white band on a red funnel made her easily recognisable.

NISBET'S *BLAIRSPEY*: A SHIP AND A HALF
Roy Fenton and Vernon Upton

War so often inflicts the extra-ordinary on the ordinary. *Blairspey* was a relatively undistinguished tramp, part of an unexceptional Glasgow fleet, until 1940.

Nisbet, Calder and Co. of Glasgow floated the Clydesdale Navigation Co. Ltd. in 1906 with a capital of £13,500, buying as its first ship the West Hartlepool-built *Greatham, ex-Bussorah* (2,338/1890). A further shipowning company, the Northern Navigation Co. Ltd. was added in 1909. Modestly capitalised at £3,300, its first purchase was the ageing *Benedick* (2,440/1890). In 1913 Calder dropped out to leave the management company as George Nisbet and Co.

All of Nisbet's ships were sold or lost during the First World War, but he returned to shipowning in 1922, probably because it was preferable to paying Excess Profits Tax on his wartime gains. A respectable fleet was quickly built up through second hand acquisitions and newbuilding, all being given names beginning *Blair,* a tradition begun when the Russian-owned *Heros* (2,549/1899) was bought and renamed *Blairhall* in 1915, and continued with such names as *Blairathol* (3,529/1924) and *Blairesk* (3,300/1925). A third shipowning company, Nisbet Shipping Co. Ltd., was added in 1924, with a nominal capital of £100,000, much larger than the earlier companies.

Nisbet specialised in trading on the North Atlantic, but also sent his ships to the White Sea, Mediterranean and occasionally to Australia. The sycophantic shipping press of the period maintained that Nisbet built up 'a fine fleet of first-class ocean-going tramps', but evidence given at the enquiry following the loss of the *Blairgowrie* in 1935 suggests that the company was cutting corners in both repairs and manning (see the caption accompanying her photograph).

The steamer *Blairspey* was delivered by the Ardrossan Dockyard Co. Ltd. in August 1929, of 4,155gt and 372 feet long with triple-expansion engines by J.G. Kincaid and Co. Ltd. of Greenock. She was one of three ordered in the late 1920s, with Nisbet no doubt believing along with some other shipowners that the post-war

The 3,260gt *Blairgowrie* was built in 1924 by Napier and Miller Ltd. at Port Glasgow for the Clydesdale Navigation Co. Ltd., Nisbet's original shipowning venture. On 16th February 1935 she left Swansea for Boston, Massachusets with a cargo of anthracite. Winds of hurricane force were met in the North Atlantic, and on 26th February *Blairgowrie* sent out distress signals in position 48.20 north by 27.01 west. Nothing further was heard from her, and she is presumed to have foundered on 27th February.

Despite the lack of survivors from her crew of 26, a court of enquiry was convened by the Wreck Commissioners and went to considerable trouble to gather evidence from those who had previously served in *Blairgowrie*. Evidence also came from letters written to his mother by chief officer Francis Warwick.

The enquiry's findings were damning. Whenever *Blairgowrie* was at sea in heavy weather, she shipped water in inexplicably large quantities. There was recurrent cracking of shell plates, and when she laboured in a seaway rivets worked loose. If the pumps were not working, water accumulated in her forepeak to considerable depths: as deep as 16 feet on occasion. A former chief officer admitted that, under the master's instructions, he had made false log entries about soundings. Repairs seem to have been ignored or botched, and the enquiry was particularly distrustful of repairs to her rod-and-chain type steering gear, which would have been under considerable strain in heavy weather. Although manning levels on *Blairgowrie* were sufficient according to Board of Trade regulations, the enquiry severely criticised the

way the men were employed. The hands were kept hard at day work on the ship in order to minimise expenditure on work done in port. This was to the detriment of the safety of the ship, as there was only one officer and a deckhand to keep the watch, and no lookouts were kept.

The enquiry's report was vehement about the failure of the owners, the officers and various Board of Trade surveyors to ensure that the ship was seaworthy and properly manned. But in the end all the court could do was to wring its hands and call for tighter regulation, because - in the absence of any direct evidence as to why the *Blairgowrie* sank - the enquiry could only speculate as to the reasons. Its report, however, was a strong indictment of the British tramp shipping industry in the 1930s. Not for the first or the last time, lives had been valued less than profits. [A. Duncan]

depression in shipping would not last much longer, and that ordering when yards were desperate for work would give him the best prices. Also from Ardrossan came *Blairnevis* (4,150/1929) and from the Ayrshire Dockyard Co. Ltd. at Irvine the *Blairmore* (4,141/1928). Of course, the improvement in freight rates was a lot longer coming than expected, and this experience made Nisbet very cautious in adding further ships. Indeed, apart from three secondhand acquisitions in the 1930s, there were to be no further additions to the fleet.

The incomplete *Blairspey* following her launch at Ardrossan in 1929. *[National Maritime Museum P9228]*

Blairspey at B&A Docks, East Boston 15th May 1932. Note the topmasts, which were never carried after her rebuild, and the partly-timbered bridge front which was replaced by a much more utilitarian structure. *[Collection of Eric Johnson, print by WA Schell]*

Thomas McCormack - second right in the photograph - was indentured as an apprentice to George Nisbet and Co. in October 1931. In return for what was supposed to be training to be an officer, he was to receive just fifty pounds for four years' labour, work which has been described by many former apprentices as virtual slave labour. Thomas's diaries for March 1933 describe the tedium of his existence. *Blairspey* was crawling across the Atlantic at just five to six knots with a cargo of coke loaded at Nordenham. The hands were put to holystoning the upper and lower bridges, and chipping the decks, despite heavy weather. The expectation of a 21-day Atlantic crossing, the never-changing routine and dreariness of the environment seems to have depressed Thomas, although he stuck it out and finished his apprenticeship, and continued to serve on *Blairspey* until 1937. His diary does establish that, at least on *Blairspey*, lookouts were posted, although evidence given to the enquiry about the loss of *Blairgowrie* suggests this was not routinely done on other Nisbet vessels. *[Mrs. J.M. McCormack]*

The slaughter of SC 7

In October 1940, *Blairspey* was homeward bound with timber from Sydney, Nova Scotia to the UK in convoy SC 7 comprising 35 merchant ships. The escort was lamentably thin, an armed yacht which left two days after leaving Sydney and the sloop HMS *Scarborough*, although an escort group of two sloops and two corvettes was due to meet the convoy. On 16th October the convoy was sighted by the German submarine *U 48*, who radioed a report to U-boat control, and attacked. Five other U-boats converged on the convoy, which had now been joined by its additional escorts, and on the calm night of 18th October under a full moon the submarines caused mayhem amongst the ships and their very green escorts. Such was the confusion that more than one submarine was often firing at the same ship, and

Admiral Dönitz credited his boats with sinking thirty ships, although more sober post-war assessments comparing German and British records brought the total down to a still very distressing twenty ships of almost 80,000 tons. Otto Kretschmer in *U 99* was credited with six and a half kills from this convoy.

In this slaughter, *Blairspey* was comparatively lucky. At 23.08 on 18th October she was hit by one or two torpedoes fired by what is believed to be *U 101* but remained afloat, although her crew abandoned her. At 02.50 the next morning she was hit twice by torpedoes from *U 100*, but still refused to sink. Undoubtedly, her timber cargo had saved the ship, but her master reported that, tragically, 18 men were lost when the forward section sank. The surviving part of *Blairspey* was taken in tow, and beached in the Clyde on

This page: the two parts of *Empire Spey* just prior to joining. The new forepart had been launched by Lithgows Ltd. as yard no. 975 on 16th February 1942. The sections were joined in the Garvel Dry Dock at Greenock. *[Glasgow University Archives]*

Opposite page: *Blairspey* in post-war years. Compared to pre-war photographs on the previous page, note the loss of the wooden bridge front and removal of the topmasts, both of which detract from her stately appearance. *[Upper: Fotoflite incorporating Skyfotos; lower: World Ship Photo Library]*

25th October. It would be interesting to know more about this epic salvage operation, which brought in half a ship abandoned in the Atlantic north west of Ireland.

With losses of the intensity of those suffered in SC 7, the UK - by now fighting alone with the Empire against Germany - was desperate for every ship, and it was decided to repair *Blairspey*. At Greenock a new bow section was built, the stern section was tidied up and the two parts joined together after being duly photographed. All this took time, and it was not until March 1942 that the ship was returned to service, now in the ownership of the Ministry of War Transport and renamed *Empire Spey*, with management by Nisbet.

The return of *Blairspey*

The end of the war found the Nisbet fleet much diminished. In addition to the casualty to *Blairspey*, no fewer than eight ships had been sunk by enemy action, two had been lost in collisions and one had disappeared. In April 1946, *Empire Spey* was sold back to her original owning company (or, more correctly, the owners of her after part) and took up her old name *Blairspey*. She went back to tramping, mainly on the North Atlantic with some visits to the West Coast of Africa. She remained a coal burner until converted to oil firing in April 1956.

Like many British tramp owners, Nisbets found life hard after the initial post-war boom. George Nisbet had died aged 65 in 1941 and his successors, no doubt chastened by the company's pre-war experience, added no new ships to those that had survived the war, and as these aged vessels were sold their fleet dwindled away. In 1961, *Blairclova* (5,102/1938) ex-*Sutherland* was sold to Hong Kong owners, leaving only *Blairspey* which soon followed her, going into flag-of-convenience ownership. She became the *Evandros* of London Greeks J.P. Hadoulis Ltd., who put under the Lebanese flag, then currently fashionable. She steamed on until broken up at Spezia in May 1967.

A lifespan of 38 years was a creditable achievement for an ordinary steam tramp, but *Blairspey* would probably not have achieved this but for her extraordinary adventures in 1940. Receiving a new forepart, she had been a ship and a half.

With *Empire Spey* to Sardinia

Vernon Upton joined *Empire Spey* as First Officer on 27th June 1944. She was in Barry Dock loading steam coal, and on 1st July sailed for the Mediterranean in convoy OS 82. At Gibraltar she joined KMS 56 which was heading for Alexandria, but *Empire Spey* was detached to head for Augusta in Sicily. Here she was given the job of acting as mother ship for a flotilla of 'Dance' class anti-submarine trawlers, including HMS *Foxtrot, Gavotte, Minuet, Polka, Quickstep, Tango,* and *Waltz.* As well as coal, *Empire Spey* carried ammunition, fresh water, and other stores for these trawlers, and it was Vernon's responsibility to liaise with the shore base and the trawlers, to ensure they were rapidly serviced. Four trawlers could be accommodated alongside *Empire Spey,* one on each side forward, and one on each side aft.

After the supply of Welsh coal had been exhausted, *Empire Spey* was ordered to Antioco in Sardinia to load local coal. The ship had no large-scale charts of the harbour entrance, and no information as to whether there were any minefields, so Antioco was entered following a ship's lifeboat, which took soundings. The Sardinians had yet to meet any Allied forces since the capitulation of Italy, and the ship was greeted by officials from Antioco and Cagliari.

Vernon gave the Sardinian stevedore instructions for loading, and when the specified tonnages in holds 2, 3 and 4 were reached, he left the Second Officer to supervise trimming by loading coal into holds 1 and 5. Early the following morning, Vernon was horrified to find the ship dramatically down by the head, with the stevedores still loading coal into hold 1, where it was running over the hatch coamings, across the deck, and even on to the dock side. The Second Officer had gone to sleep, and left the stevedores to it.

Orders had to be issued to discharge the surplus coal from hold 1, pile it high on the dockside, and move the ship so that the surplus coal could be loaded in hold 5 to trim the ship correctly. After that episode, Captain Rush and Vernon decided not to allow the Second or Third Officers to be unsupervised, and they doubled up the watches from then on, both in port and at sea.

Empire Spey returned to Augusta to resume duty as a mother ship for the trawlers, later moving to Bari and then Barletta in the Adriatic. From there, the ship was sent to Bone in Algeria, to load iron ore, sailing in convoy MKS 630 and joining SC 132 at Gibraltar. She arrived home in Glasgow on 16th October 1944.

Empire Spey in wartime. David Hodge of the National Maritime Museum has carried out some very careful detective work to identify the location. From the ports *Empire Spey* is known to have visited between 1942 and 1946, David used maps and postcards to establish that it was most likely Huelva, and that *Empire Spey* is alongside the Muelle Definitivo. The trawlers alongside suggested that it might show one of the Sardinian or Sicilian ports which Vernon Upton visited in *Empire Spey,* but those in the photograph are mercantile rather than naval. David concludes that the photograph was taken during a visit to Huelva in October 1943, but he and the editors of *Record* would welcome any evidence for or against this conclusion. *[National Maritime Museum P22466]*

RECORD BOOKS
'SHIP RECOGNITION' BY LAURENCE DUNN
Stephen Howells

Unlike books previously featured in this occasional column, Laurence Dunn's 'Ship Recognition' has not influenced the historiography of shipping, but it has seriously affected the history of at least one ship watcher, the author. My first shipping books, the estimable and much imitated ABC series from Ian Allan, were long on names, dimensions and ownership, but they were short on the anatomy of ships themselves. However, the bookshops of Liverpool came up with an affordable, attractive and highly accessible source of such information in Laurence Dunn's little hardback.

Laurence's intention, expressed in his preface, was '...to clothe the distant ship with name and family, origin and history...' He recommended achieving this by careful analysis of the vessel's hull, superstructure and general layout, and by seeking tell-tale fittings which betray age, purpose, and often nationality and ownership. The author sought to instruct his pupils not by a complex, formulaic approach, as adopted by his near-contemporary Talbot-Booth, but through a combination of lucid descriptions and clear drawings. He started with the simplest coasters, the easiest vessels for the novice to practice on, and worked systematically up to the largest ships, taking first those with engines aft (of which surprisingly few seem to have been around at the time the third edition became available in 1961) and then those with machinery amidships. One of those arbitrary divisions which shipping authors adopt saw the deep-sea freighter and the cargo liner separated. The former category, essentially covering tramps, did have one of the book's most useful sections for me, distinguishing the various Second World War-built standard cargo ships which were still greatly in evidence in the early 1960s.

The pattern of each chapter is a short but clear description of typical ships, using real examples rather than idealised ships, illustrated by drawings in several different styles. There follows several pages of photographs, each accompanied with an extensive discussion of what to look for.

Fascinating small details are brought out: for instance, the deep white panel around the stern of Dutch but not British examples of Shell's ubiquitous 18,000 ton tankers; the radiused edge to the decks of certain Scandinavian tankers. These are clearly the results of careful personal observation of ships. Undoubtedly, Laurence Dunn was ideally placed to produce 'Ship Recognition'. A practising artist, he could draw the profiles to bring out the point he was making in the text, and could write with sympathy and understanding of the way a ship looks - the benefits of an artist's eye. He is also an accomplished photographer, although the credits make it clear that not all the photographs used are from his camera.

Revisiting 'Ship Recognition' forty years on, the impression is of a huge amount of valuable information concisely but elegantly packed into 132 small pages. As well as that hallmark of a proper book, an index, there is an illustrated glossary, an explanation of tonnage measurements, plus several pages of diagrams and photos of hull forms, bows, sterns, masts, funnels and ventilators.

An indication of both the author's thoroughness and his comprehensive knowledge of ships is that no half-way important ship type seems excluded, and no major national type ignored. An example is the Liberty collier, mentioned though not illustrated, and classed as '...rarely, if ever, seen outside US waters.' This young enthusiast took immense

satisfaction in identifying, from Laurence's description, two of these exotic vagrants which turned up in Birkenhead docks in the 1960s.

I, and certainly some of my contemporaries, learned much shipping terminology from Laurence's book. Who else would have told us that the bulwark plating alongside a change in level of deck, and which had such an effect on the look of a ship, was known as a hance? And who but he would have informed us that the scrap of raised bulwark plating right in the bow was a spirket plate, which we learned in later years to be a most important feature when identifying unkown ships in photographs.

As practically all the ships featured are long gone from the seas, and the present generation of ships have very little in common with those they replaced, 'Ship Recognition' is no longer of much help as a recognition manual. This begs the question, would a new version be useful? Although ships have altered vastly since the early 1960s, there is probably as much variation as ever between individual designs. Even amongst the ubiquitous engines-aft bulk carrier, there are geared and gearless variants, size differences, and variations in superstructure and funnel design. The fact that yards now often build to standard designs makes the sport of ship recognition that much more interesting: think of the scope for identifying who built a particular coaster, and especially distinguishing between all the designs from Sietas. National characteristics are also often apparent; for instance, the series-built vessels for the former USSR which were not featured in the original book. And as Peter Wynne's series of articles in *Record* are showing, even amongst an apparently homogenous group of ships such as the ORSVS there are differences in appearance which belie individual function, discerning which can add greatly to the enjoyment of shipwatching.

It is a credit to Laurence's thorough analytical approach that an entirely new version on the same lines would be an excellent asset. At the very least, it might help inspire the interest of people of the age the author was when he lighted on 'Ship Recognition', youngsters of a generation who mostly seem to disdain an interest in the romantic, often distant but also highly individual objects that are ships.

THE HANSA A TYPE

Of the several standard German types of the Second World War, the *Hansa A* was the most numerous (see Fig. 36 and RICHARD BORCHARD, p. 52). Over sixty were built, both in German yards and those of the occupied countries. These 1,900-ton fo'c'sle type ships have two hatches forward and one aft. Two king-posts are placed at the front of the bridge with a further pair (or a single one) aft. Distinctive features are the bulwarks on the after deckhouse and the fact that the deck by the lifeboats is not full hull width. These successful and popular ships are now widely distributed under many flags, but few have undergone much alteration.

THE SMALLER
REGULAR TRADER

Ships mentioned so far are mostly tramps, while the regular traders are generally of more modern construction. Various cargoes are the rule for these, so that the provision of a second deck is necessary. The open shelter deck arrangement is thus very popular, providing good cubic capacity on the minimum tonnage. These ships mostly have a flush weather deck, with perhaps a raised fo'c'sle or bridge deck. Smaller ships have three hatches, two forward and one aft of the superstructure. As seen in CORVUS and LAVEROCK (p. 51) the mainmast may be either ahead or astern of No. 3 hatch. Derricks are often supplemented by cranes.

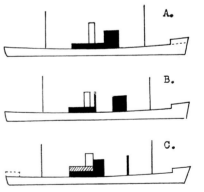

FIG. 37: *A.* Low composite superstructure between two pairs of hatches.
B. Superstructure split to take extra hatch between bridge and funnel.
C. Superstructure made shorter and taller than *A* to allow for longer third hatch forward of bridge.

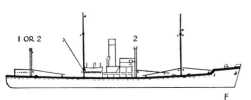

FIG. 36: German *Hansa A* type steamer, built 1943–5. 1,900 tons gross, 3,200 d.w., length 302 ft. Speed 10½ knots.

SMALL EUROPE–GREAT
LAKES SHIPS

Many rather larger ships, with four hatches—two forward and two aft of the

LOOSE ENDS

The editors warmly welcome readers' photographs which depict ships which have had a significant mention in *Record,* but where we have been unable to find a photograph, or not been able to locate one in the name or ownership under which she is featured. We are also pleased to receive any other interestingly different photographs of the ship in question, particularly if it is depicted in wartime colours or is experiencing some dramatic event, or indeed anything which complements our features. A number of such shots have accumulated, relating to features which go back almost until *Records* began. We are very grateful to all who sent photographs.

South African coasters (*Record* 8)
Swazi Coast, shown opposite top, had a life that belied her tiny size: she was just under 100 feet long, yet managed an epic delivery voyage, and at the end of her career it took both ships and aircraft of South Africa's armed forces to lay her to rest. She was completed in November 1927 at *Swazi* at Yarwood's yard on the River Weaver in Cheshire. Her delivery voyage was aborted when she had reached no further than the Irish Sea, putting into Holyhead with her bilges choked. Eventually arriving at Cape Town, after what must have been an epic voyage in such a small vessel, she was registered locally in the ownership of Thesen's Steamship Co. Ltd., for whom she was put into service between Cape Town, Port Nolloth and Lambert's Bay. During the war her shallow draft won her several jobs

salvaging cargo from ships wrecked off South Africa, including Ellerman's *City of Hankow* (7,369/1915) and the Liberty *Thomas T. Tucker* (7,176/1942), from which she extracted Sherman tanks bound for Egypt.

The photograph was taken in June 1953, soon after the takeover of Thesens by Coast Lines resulted in her being renamed *Swazi Coast.* It seems likely that she retained the open wheelhouse until the end of her life in 1958.

Possibly because of the lack of a local scrap industry, she was not broken up but taken out of Cape Town and expended as a target. After a South African frigate had a go at her, she was finished off by depth charges from a South African Air Force Shackleton. Thanks to Clive Guthrie for details of her career. *[J. and M. Clarkson]*

Natal Coast (3,078/1920) (opposite lower, taken June 1954) was an altogether more sizeable and robust coaster, but again one that had an interesting life. She was laid down at Dublin Dockyard as *War Cloud* for the Shipping Controller, but on completion in May 1920 had been sold to the Limerick Steamship Co. Ltd. as *Glenstal.* Within months she was sailing for Australia, to become the *Aldinga* of the Adelaide Steamship Co. Ltd. Then followed 32 years of stability, until sold in 1952 to the Neptune Shipping Co (Pty) Ltd., Durban who gave her the name *Natal Coast.* But it was only carried for three years: on 30th April 1955 *Natal Coast* was wrecked south of Walvis Bay whilst on a voyage from Matadi to Table Bay and Durban with timber and palm oil. *[J. and M. Clarkson]*

POLSKAROB (*Record* 13)
Although it was almost a year since peace had broken out in Europe, *Kmicic* (1,138/1923) still wears grey and carries Carley floats in this view at Blyth in April 1946 (above). Originally the Newcastle-owned *Akenside,* she had been *Robur III* for Polish collier owners POLSKAROB between 1928 and 1940. Following the occupation of Poland, manager Alfred Falter established himself first in France. He renamed the ship *Kmicic* and she came under British control following the fall of France, when Falter escaped to New York. After a number of wartime adventures, including shooting down several Dorniers and being the first Allied ship to re-enter Ghent, *Kmicic* was

handed back to Falter in November 1946 and became *Chopin* under the Panama flag. Note the splendid paddle tug *Earl of Beaconsfield* (114/1889) of the Blyth Tug Co. Ltd. *[Laurence Dunn]*

In the article on POLSKAROB, *Robur V* (1,975/1930) was depicted under this, her original name, and as *Copernicus,* which name she took when owned in New York after 1946. Above she is seen with the

intermediate name *Kordeki,* carried from 1940 to 1946 when she was under British control and, like *Kmicic,* managed by William Cory and Son Ltd. *[National Maritime Museum 60/138]*

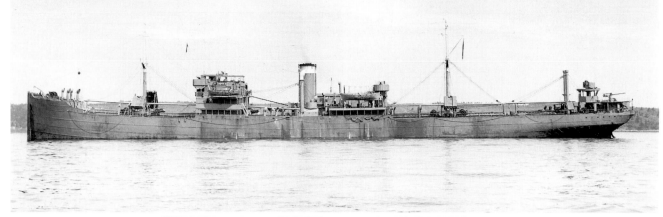

Furness North Pacific Ships
(*Records* 14 and 15)
More wartime views supplement the articles on the ships which maintained the Furness service from Pacific ports of North America to the UK. The conifers in the background suggest that the Doxford motorship *Pacific Shipper* (top) is in Canadian waters. Note the white tops to masts and funnel - presumably to prevent them standing out against the sky - and the name 'P Shipper' displayed on the board on the bridge. *Pacific Shipper* (6,304/1924) survived the war and was broken up at Briton Ferry in 1950. *[National Maritime Museum P23722]*

The United States Coast Guard got into the habit of photographing most foreign ships entering US ports whilst their country was neutral, and continued even when the US entered the war and the foreign ships became allies. This resulted in a rich archive of wartime views, in some cases including the only known photos of short-lived vessels. The motorship *Pacific Pioneer* (6,723/1928) was photographed (right upper) on 17th January 1942, little over five weeks after the USA had entered the war. *Pacific Pioneer* was sunk later that year, torpedoed by *U 132* on 29th July 1942. *[Courtesy John Hill]*

Taken a few days later, the lower above depicts *Pacific Grove* (7,114/1928) outbound on 22nd January 1942. She had already had an adventurous time. Her lifeboats were used to lift troops off the beaches at Dunkirk, and she survived an attack by a Focke Wulf Condor, when a 500lb bomb failed to explode and was manhandled over the side. Her luck ran out on 12th April 1943 when she was torpedoed by *U 563* whilst homeward bound in convoy HX 232. *[Courtesy John Hill]*

Harrison four-masters (*Record* 16)
When we compiled this feature, photographs had not been found of four of this group of 22 ships. Two of these gaps have now been filled.

Third of the four-masters, *Workman* (6,116/1898) was wrecked of Rio de Janeiro on 26th December 1912. Making up for her absence from the original article, this slightly faded photograph (right) shows *Workman* tied up somewhere along the Suez Canal waiting for other ships to pass; note the searchlight mounted on her bow. *[Ian Harmsworth]*

Two photographs have come along of the first *Huntsman* (7,460/1904). The lower is interesting in showing her carrying a number reminiscent of those distinguishing transports in the Boer War, for which conflict *Huntsman* was completed too late. However, this photograph is believed to show her in the Red Sea in 1914, carrying an Indian Lancer regiment. Note what could well be horse stalls in the wells and the canvas ventilators to the holds. With a following wind, it was sometimes necessary to turn about and steam in the opposite direction to force enough air into the holds for the horses.

Huntsman was torpedoed and sunk by *U 50* in the Atlantic on 25th February 1917. *[National Maritime Museum P16945 and P16947]*

Defender (8,078/1915) was the last survivor of the four-masters, and although well illustrated in *Record* 16, these fine photographs taken on the Scheldt on 4th November 1945 are interesting in showing her in wartime condition apart from her funnel and the addition of names in small black letters. *Defender* is certainly well defended: six guns can be seen. *[Flor Van Otterdyk]*

Readhead's Cliffe Steamship Co. Ltd. (*Record* 19)

Two of the ships owned by this subsidiary of shipbuilder John Readhead escaped depiction by photographs in this article, and readers have made up for this. The company's first ship, *Rockcliffe* (1) (3,073/1904), is seen left, probably on trials or her first voyage. She was sunk by a German cruiser in the Black Sea on 27th September 1916. *[George Scott collection]*

Readheads built *Ulidia* (3,081/1903) for Newry owners Joseph Fisher and Sons, and she is seen (below) in their colours, probably in an Eastern Mediterranean port. *Ulidia* represented something of a speculation by Fishers in the tramp trades, as she was much to big for her home port, and for Fisher's normal business of running cargoes of coal from the Mersey and elsewhere to Newry and other Irish ports. Fishers sold *Ulidia* back to Readheads, who operated her under ownership by the Cliffe Steamship Co. Ltd. from 1916 until she stranded in the White Sea in September 1919. After repairs, she sailed under Norwegian, Chinese, Dutch, US and (again) Chinese flags before being wrecked in June 1948. *[Terry O'Conallain collection]*

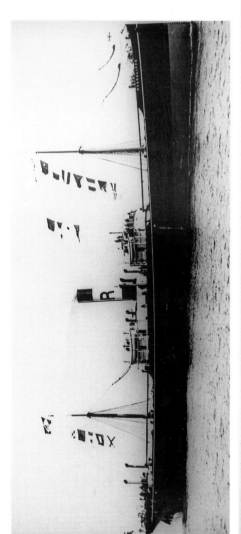

Orkney shipowners - William and Peter Cooper (*Record* 19)

The middle of the three David MacBrayne ships shown opposite in the Caledonian Canal is *Clansman* (265/1880), which was owned by the Coopers of Kirkwall between 1918 and 1920. She had been built as *Ethel* and renamed *Clansman* in October 1910, dating this view to the years just before the First World War. After her Orkney ownership she had a number of owners on the east coast of England, and foundered off Haisboro' in October 1924.

Glengarry (124/1844), to the right, is a real veteran. She was built back in 1844 as the *Edinburgh Castle* for the Holy Loch service of the Glasgow Castles Steam Packet Company. After just a year she gravitated to the Caledonian Canal, where she stayed, being rebuilt in 1875 and renamed *Glengarry*. She lasted until 1927, when she was broken up in her home port of Inverness. Her hull surviving this long was remarkable enough, but seemingly her original, single-cylinder steeple engine was still in place after 83 years.

The star of this photograph, however, is MacBrayne's *Gondolier* (173/1866). For 70 years she maintained a service between Inverness and Banavie, leaving the canal only for refits on the Clyde, and for her last resting place, the waters of the Orkneys where the Admiralty used her hull to block one of the entrances to Scapa Flow. *[Roy Fenton collection]*

British liners - Greek tramps (*Record* 19)

John Lingwood's article on shipbuilders of the lower Wear and their products prompted Ian Rae to send this splendid photograph of a Wear-built ship in war paint, the *War Climax* (6,429/1918) on trials from Swan, Hunter's Sunderland yard in October 1918. But the

photograph could equally well complement Malcolm Cooper's article on British cargo liners which were sold off cheaply to Greek tramp operators. On page 140 of issue 19, *War Climax* appears as *Rokos*, her fourth name, the intermediate names being *Glenstrae* and *Banbury Castle*. Her fate as *Rokos* is discussed in some depth

in 'Putting the Record straight' in issue 21. *[Ian Rae]*
Ian sent another excellent photograph of shipbuilding activity on the Wear, but we are holding this in anticipation of a further article by John Lingwood on the yards of the upper Wear.